EDITED BY
AMITH PRABHU
AND
SARIKA CHAVAN

SHINE

STORIES AND INSIGHTS FROM INDIA'S PUBLIC RELATIONS BUILDERS

WESTLAND
BUSINESS

WESTLAND
BUSINESS

Published by Westland Business, an imprint of Westland Books, a division of Nasadiya Technologies Private Limited, in 2025

No. 269/2B, First Floor, 'Irai Arul', Vimalraj Street, Nethaji Nagar, Alapakkam Main Road, Maduravoyal, Chennai 600095

ISBN: 9789360451981

10 9 8 7 6 5 4 3 2 1

Typeset by Mukul

Printed at Thomson Press (India) Ltd

SHINE

Amith Prabhu is a pioneering Public Relations and reputation management professional with over twenty years of experience. He has worked in India and in the USA at leading marketing communication companies. He is the co-founder of India's only weekend offsite summit for the profession, PRAXIS. He serves on the international board of the Global Alliance (GA). He is the founding dean at the School of Communications & Reputation (SCoRe) in Mumbai. He has a postgraduate degree in Public Relations and communication management from Symbiosis Institute of Media and Communication. He lives in Gurgaon. He can be found on Twitter @amithpr.

Sarika Chavan is the founder of Sparkle Gift Cards and the director of social impact at The PRomise Foundation. She is a Public Relations professional with over nineteen years of work experience. Her last stint was at Weber Shandwick Mumbai, where she was vice president—client experience. Previously she was employed at Adfactors PR, Text100 (now known as Archetype) and Perfect Relations. She writes the longest-running monthly book review column. She has a postgraduate diploma from the Xavier Institute of Communications. She lives in Mumbai. She can be found on Twitter @sourikka.

We would like to dedicate this book to our daughters because we know they will Shine

Sarika's daughters Sia and Saisha

and Amith's daughter Swara

Contents

INTRODUCTION

THIS BOOK IS A SEQUEL TO THE FIRST IN THE SERIES, *SPARK*, which was published in November 2024. That book carried the stories of twenty-four pioneers of Indian public relations, mostly founders. This book has a set of thirty leaders who built on some of those foundations. These professionals include some founders and several chief executives who have taken the profession ahead in the last decade.

We hope you have read *Spark* already. The stories that you read in this book are equally inspiring. We invited thirty-five leaders to write, of which thirty feature here. Five preferred to continue to inspire through their work rather than being written about. Two of these—Amit Misra and Jaideep Shergill—have been mentors at different stages to Amith. Further, we decided to hold on to some professionals who are still building an enterprise or are less than twenty years in the profession for a later project.

Work on this book began as soon as the previous one was completed. The same process was followed for the most part. An interview was followed by the transcription, which was then refined further. In some cases, we used previous interviews we had done to put together the piece. We also invited each of them to write two short essays. The first was on the evolution of PR in the years gone by and the second on the future of PR. Some did, while some chose not to. For those who did, the second part of each chapter includes their write-up. The third essay will reside on the online portal: lightaspark.online.

We are glad that Westland accepted our idea. These perspectives are a must-read for any aspiring PR professional looking to become an effective leader and wanting to learn from the best. This is also a must-read for anyone who is part of the profession and didn't know how someone made it in the field of PR.

We have ensured two words do not feature in our writing—'agency' and 'industry'. 'Industry' because it is a wrong way to refer to our profession. Do lawyers and management consultants say they are from an industry? 'Agency' because PR firms are modelled around law firms, which charge a project fee or a retainer fee and not a commission like agencies do. We hope you appreciate this perspective.

We are working on the third in the series focused on more than forty chief communication officers. Over time, we hope this initiative will grow into multiple facets, including a conclave that will inspire the next generation of PR professionals.

It is our hope that this book will motivate, shape and empower you in some way, perhaps even making you a better person or professional. This is a passion project from us to the PR community and to those who wish to learn from the journeys of those who came before them.

We are glad you are reading this book, which we believe will go a long way in documenting the history of Indian PR.

1

Kiran Ray Chaudhary

Co-founder and Joint Managing Director, 80 dB Communications

'Over the years, I've worn many hats, and the discipline and sense of community I've built along the way have been invaluable.'

From Journalism to Public Relations Entrepreneurship

My dad was a pilot in the Indian Air Force. He flew the transport fleet and was the first commanding officer of the Ilyushin Il-76. I was born in 1973 in Bareilly. My limited connection to the town stems from the fact that my grandparents lived there. As a defence kid, I moved around a lot—my dad was posted in places like Chandigarh, Agra, Delhi, Wellington, Udhampur and Shillong. So, except for the first seven or eight years in Chandigarh, we were constantly on the move. In class nine, I joined Air Force Bal Bharti School in New Delhi and moved into its hostel. My brother, too, went to a hostel. The idea was to give us a more stable schooling experience in our senior years, avoiding the disruptions caused by frequent relocations. My brother, who is two years older than me, is now a Brigadier in the Army.

After school, I went to Lady Shri Ram College for an English honours degree. Throughout school, I had a strong interest in literature and journalism, and I aimed to pursue a career in those fields. After obtaining my bachelor's degree, I joined a master's programme, considering a future as either an academic or a journalist.

After obtaining my master's degree, I was hired as a journalist by a television production house that created a business programme for Doordarshan. I had a great experience working as part of a small team. I had the opportunity to be on camera, report on stories, and even sit with the editor to edit my own stories. I remember the first story I wrote entirely on my own. My editor changed everything except for the first word.

While working in television, I met several PR professionals. Besides, I had friends who worked at Perfect Relations and IPAN, so I was not unfamiliar with that field. As a journalist, I was often overwhelmed by their warmth and interest in me. When the production house I worked for began facing financial difficulties within a few months of my joining, I reached out to someone I'd met at a conference who got me an interview with Sunil, the founder of 20:20 Media. I was hired on the spot, and I've never looked back since then.

I quickly adapted to the world of PR. I loved the energy and everything I was learning from day one. I was the fourth member of a small team at 2020 Media (now 2020 MSL). It turned out to be an incredible experience, and I was hooked from the start.

Looking back, I realise how much my experience in those early years shaped my career. That is why I want anyone who joins us today to have a similar experience—one filled with learning, a sense of belonging to a team and the excitement of working on new and sometimes even crazy ideas together. We tried new things, executed innovative concepts and grew together as a team.

Our boss at the time, Sunil Agarwal, an IIT graduate and an IIM-A alumnus, was a great mentor. I vividly remember him dedicating an entire day to teaching us how to think like a business major in only twenty-four hours—this is just one example of the invaluable insights he shared with us. His efforts to invest in our development were remarkable, and the clients we worked with only added to the richness of my experience.

I spent almost twelve years at 20:20 Media, and then took a break. My plan was to take a two-year sabbatical and spend time with my daughter, who was three at the time. However, life had other plans. Instead of the break, I found myself diving into entrepreneurship. At that time, friends had begun to reach out, asking if I could help handle the PR for their projects. Soon, I was involved in a few ventures that required me to formalise the set-up for taxation reasons.

Around this time, I reconnected with some old acquaintances, who were also looking for flexible work opportunities, and we decided to join forces. What began with just me and my colleague Priya Bellani (who continues to be at 80 dB now) quickly grew into Aether Marketing, a company I ran for seven years, with a focus on high-impact marketing solutions. We kept our client list small on purpose, but each project was significant both in scale and value.

We were fortunate to work on some amazing projects with major companies. In the final year of Aether, Abhilasha Padhy joined the team after taking on freelance work post-maternity leave. Together, we expanded into PR services. However, after about fourteen months, Abhilasha received an opportunity with Google and decided to move on.

I like to tease Abhilasha that the entrepreneurial bug had bitten her too, and we started talking seriously about working on a venture together. That conversation eventually led to the creation of 80 dB. We had been casually discussing it for a while without making my concrete plans, when, out of the blue, our first client reached out and said, 'I want you to take on my business.' That was the push we needed to formalise our business and get the ball rolling.

By April 2015, we had incorporated and officially launched 80 dB. From there started the journey of building our team and expanding our client base.

While 2020 Media was India's tech-first PR firm, from the very beginning, 80 dB embraced a sector-agnostic approach. We work across diverse industries, including retail, hospitality, auto and e-commerce. This versatility comes naturally to us, and we have developed communications expertise across platforms for different sector requirements.

Our approach to any mandate starts with aligning business objectives with communication goals, which are then translated into the brand's core messages. From there, we choose the appropriate mediums to deliver those messages—whether it's through traditional media, digital, social, or influencers—based on the brand's needs.

Over the years, we've expanded into managing founders and CEOs on social platforms and built a thriving influencer practice, working with a variety of hospitality and beauty brands. Our focus has always been on helping brands achieve their business objectives through communications, and the strategy flows from there.

For example, in the case of Fabindia, the corporate mandate was to focus on reaching a new demographic—users who weren't already fans of the brand but were potential customers. This required a completely different strategy, with influencers playing a central role in reaching and engaging this audience.

PR is constantly evolving, and staying ahead of trends keeps us competitive. Many of the services we excel at today—like influencer marketing and social media strategy—were developed over the past few years as we saw new opportunities and took them head on, learning and building our expertise as we grew. By working with brands across various sectors, we've gained deep expertise and competencies in diverse areas.

While clients may not always invest in full-service mandates due to budget constraints, we still aim for a holistic view of each one. Our approach is always integrated. Competencies within the firm are growing as well, with traditional PR professionals gradually expanding their skill sets towards more integrated communication strategies. But this transformation takes time and experience.

I've worked on countless memorable campaigns. While the smaller, day-to-day ones are equally valuable, it's the peak moments that really stand out and teach you the most. These lessons are much more important than the campaign itself.

One of the most valuable lessons comes from managing crisis campaigns. You never know how far you'll be stretched, and these situations can be moments of self-discovery, where you realise your capacity to handle challenges.

One of the significant ways this lesson has impacted my personal life is when, in my early forties, I took up running marathons. Looking back, I realise I trained hard for my first marathon to prove to myself that if I set my mind to something, I could achieve it. It became about pushing my own boundaries and testing my limits.

Similarly, in crisis situations or even in new ventures—like managing social media for founders—the experience has been a huge learning curve. As we've developed and expanded these practices, they have provided valuable insights into what we can achieve and how we can continuously push ourselves to grow.

The past nine years have been a great ride—time has flown by. But looking back, I realise that the experiences, learnings, relationships and projects that came before 80 dB have all contributed to our success. Those years prepared me to take on the challenges of entrepreneurship with confidence.

Also, the fact that I am from a defence family has played a role in shaping my approach. When you're going through it, you may not fully appreciate it, but in hindsight I can see how my decisions—like staying long term in roles—were influenced by that atmosphere. My father had a forty-year career with the Indian Air Force, and perhaps that sense of commitment and stability has stayed with me as well.

I'm grateful for the long stints I've had in various places. Over the years, I've worn many hats, and the discipline and sense of community I've built along the way have been invaluable. The relationships I've cultivated over the past twenty years, even before starting 80 dB, have been instrumental in supporting us and pushing us towards success. That includes my former boss, who I still stay in touch with and speak to often.

I have had the opportunity to work on numerous projects, each presenting its own unique challenges and rewards. From visits from international CEOs, a memorable one being Carly Fiorina, the CEO of HP, to a CIO study for Citrix Systems (which was also a first for the firm), to launching new start-ups at 80 dB, designing and curating events for Google and handling crisis communications for brands, especially during COVID-19, the list is endless. I'd like to share some of the key lessons that have emerged from these—and other—experiences. In this field, it's crucial to plan meticulously while also being ready for the unexpected. I've learnt that no matter how well you plan, things can always go wrong—like a last-minute keynote speaker cancellation or an unforeseen technical issue. Being ready to adapt quickly has been vital in managing these high-pressure situations. Staying calm and maintaining composure often make all the difference.

Attention to detail is another key aspect. I recall a significant event where a last-minute check revealed a mistake in the stage backdrop design—a potential crisis that we managed to avert just in time. Experiences like this have reinforced the importance of thorough preparation and careful oversight.

Managing diverse teams and coordinating with multiple stakeholders—clients, partners and internal teams—has also been both a challenge and a rewarding experience. It's about understanding different expectations and finding a balance that satisfies everyone involved while keeping the project's goals in focus. Effective communication and clear direction have been essential in leading teams through these complex projects.

PR requires quick thinking and, consequently, the ability to pivot strategies as conditions change, whether due to market shifts or internal dynamics within a client's organisation. Being flexible while keeping an eye on the bigger picture helps to navigate these turns successfully.

Trust is at the heart of any successful partnership, and consistently delivering value helps to build and maintain it over time. Moreover, always measuring and evaluating our initiatives' impact allows us to learn, refine and improve our strategies, ensuring we deliver meaningful results.

Many lessons in PR are best learnt on the job, through experience. There's really no substitute to this; this is where the muscle is honed.

The Shifting Landscape

The evolution of PR over the last twenty years can best be encapsulated by the adage: The more things change, the more they remain the same. While the tools, channels and strategies have evolved dramatically, the core principles of PR remain timeless. Some things have changed though.

Mediums and platforms: The explosion of digital and social media channels has fundamentally transformed how news and information are consumed. Twenty years ago, traditional media dominated the PR landscape. Today, platforms like Instagram, LinkedIn, Reddit and X have emerged as critical spaces for storytelling and reputation management. Their rise has diversified the mediums of communication and also amplified the speed and reach of messaging. News can go viral in minutes, making agility and vigilance more important than ever for PR professionals.

Changing demographics and news consumption habits: The ways in which people engage with information have shifted dramatically too. Younger audiences are more likely to seek information from influencers, community-driven platforms and direct brand communications than traditional outlets. Hence, a shift in PR strategies to include not just earned media but also owned and shared media platforms. Moreover, this change has given rise to segmentation in targeting audiences. There is no longer a one-size-fits-all approach; each demographic or niche group demands tailored messaging and platform-specific strategies.

The blurring of paid, earned and owned media: The traditional silos of these three are dissolving. Today's mandates often require an integrated approach, where a campaign might simultaneously leverage earned media for credibility, owned media for depth and paid media for amplification. This interplay demands that PR professionals be adept at strategising across multiple domains.

Individual credibility and leadership profiles: A noticeable shift is the increasing importance of personal branding for leaders, especially CEOs. Building and maintaining individual credibility has become a core focus of PR strategies, with leaders often serving as the face of their organisations. Authenticity and visibility on social platforms are now prerequisites for effective leadership communication.

However, some things do remain the same.

Reputation as the cornerstone: At its heart, PR has always been about safeguarding and enhancing reputation. This fundamental principle hasn't changed, only the stakes have grown higher in a world where reputational damage can spread within hours.

The value of human relationships: Despite advancements in technology and AI, the essence of PR lies in relationships—understanding clients deeply, building trust with journalists and fostering connections with audiences.

Creativity and attention to detail: The ability to craft compelling narratives and execute them flawlessly has always set great PR professionals apart. These skills continue to be highly valued, even as the mediums for storytelling evolve.

While technology has not replaced the human touch, it has become an indispensable enabler. AI and data analytics are being leveraged to identify trends, measure impact and combat misinformation. Machine learning tools help PR practitioners monitor narratives in real time, enabling swift responses to emerging crises.

PR's role within the broader communications and marketing ecosystem has grown more pronounced. The blurring lines between marketing, branding and PR mean that we must now deliver integrated strategies that tie directly to business goals. Good ideas are no longer confined to any one discipline—they can come from anywhere—and PR is increasingly expected to lead this charge.

Internal communication is gaining prominence as organisations recognise the power of employees as brand ambassadors. This trend highlights the need for a cohesive narrative that resonates both internally and externally.

2

Madhvendra Das

Founder Director, The Good Edge

'Studying history was incredibly enlightening and shaped the way I approach everything—with reasoning and critical thinking.'

From Journalism to Corporate Communication to Building a Consultancy

I was born in Fatehpur, located between Allahabad and Kanpur, right on the Grand Trunk Road, in Uttar Pradesh. I come from a family of lawyers. My father, however, switched careers in the early 1960s and took up a job instead. As a result, I spent my first six to eight months in Kolkata, before moving to Allahabad.

In Allahabad, we lived near the banks of the river Ganga. I have distinct memories of my grandfather taking me on daily boat tours of the river, especially during the monsoon when the rising water would reach the basement of our house. I was only around three years old at the time, but I remember taking the boat right from the steps of our house and going on these little excursions with him. Since our family was also very religious, I grew up with a strong sense of that influence and it shaped a lot of my early years.

In early 1972, when I was about four years old, my father was transferred to Delhi. Living in the big city was a whole new experience—coming from a large, isolated house in Allahabad to a small home in a Delhi colony filled with children was quite a shock. But I warmed up to it soon enough and quite enjoyed it.

I studied at Bharati Air Force School till the sixth standard. In 1978, my father was transferred to Patna, where he joined the State Bank of India, marking the beginning of a new chapter. We lived there till 1991, and I completed my tenth grade at Loyola High School.

After that, I returned to Delhi to finish my senior schooling at Delhi Public School, RK Puram, and at Hans Raj College, Delhi University, where I studied history for both my BA and MA degrees. The way history was taught at Delhi University was quite different from school—it wasn't just about dates and kings but about the life and times of civilisations. It involved a deeper, multidimensional understanding, often requiring forensics to piece together ancient history. You had to corroborate and cross-check facts, as many records were written by court historians, who often exaggerated the truth.

Studying history was incredibly enlightening and shaped the way I approach everything—with reasoning and critical thinking. It taught me not to accept things blindly but to explore multiple sources for verification. Although I didn't know it at the time, I was unknowingly preparing myself for a career in journalism. The study of history was fascinating, especially when we explored various theories like feudalism and capitalism. I was intrigued by the concept of the 'prime mover', the tipping point or trigger factor that led to the fall of a kingdom or a shift in modes of production. Understanding these turning points in history captivated me, and this approach to identifying critical moments that change the course of events has proven valuable in my life.

While pursuing my master's degree in history, I also attempted the civil services exam, which is somewhat of a national pastime. To be honest, I wasn't sure what I'd get out of it and didn't put in as much effort as I could have. Obviously, it didn't quite work out. Luckily, by the end of 1991, my father was transferred to Mumbai, and I moved there the next year. Having completed my master's in history, job prospects in Mumbai seemed limited, so I secured a job in sales. Soon, I joined Modi GBC Limited, a sister concern of Modi Xerox, which sold binding, laminating and shredding machines made by the American General Binding Corporation. It was part of the document industry, and I discovered there that I had a knack for sales which got honed by the legendary training of Xerox.

Two years later, in 1994, I realised that if I wanted to continue in the private sector, I would need further qualifications. A master's in history wouldn't be enough, so I decided to get an MBA degree. I got through the MMS (Masters in Management Studies) programme at the Narsee Monjee Institute of Management. Initially, I planned to major in marketing because of my sales background, but when I started the programme, I found the world of finance fascinating. Financial management, with its strong logic and base in facts and their analysis, was incredibly appealing. I enjoyed analysing a balance sheet to discern the health and future prospects of a business, how to assess a project's success and the overall decision-making process in finance. So, despite having no background in finance or commerce, I decided to major in it.

By 1996, India was going through its second financial crisis, the MS Shoes scandal, and job opportunities in financial services were shrinking. I joined a boutique investment bank that focused on merchant banking and short-tenor corporate lending. There, I created quarterly economy reports for clients, possibly preparing myself further for a career in journalism. It was around this time that I had a meeting with the editors at *The Economic Times*. At the end of an illuminating conversation, they offered me a role as a research analyst in their banking bureau. India had recently entered the liberalisation phase, and there was a lot of change happening in financial services, banking and investment banking. *The Economic Times* wanted someone with industry experience to help explain these changes in simpler terms. I joined the publication, writing about financial services, investment banking, and development finance.

Towards the end of the millennium, ICICI was transforming from a development financial institution into a commercial bank, and they were looking to set up a corporate communications division. They approached me to help establish it, and at the age of thirty-one, I joined ICICI in January 2000, marking the beginning of my journey into corporate communications and public relations.

At that time, ICICI was undergoing a significant transformation and had some of the most influential leaders of the financial world, including K.V. Kamath, Lalita Gupte, Kalpana Morparia, Subrata Mukherji, Shikha Sharma, Chanda Kochhar, Nachiket Mor, Madhabi Puri Buch, Renuka Ramnath, Vishakha Mulye, V. Vaidyanathan, Amitabh

Chaturvedi and Rajiv Sabharwal. I had the opportunity to interact with all of them. This fascinating period of learning allowed me to build important connections in the media world. Concepts like retail finance and EMIs were new, and everyone—journalists and communications persons—were adapting and growing.

I spent about five-and-a-half years at ICICI, during which I lived through a few major crises and large transactions, including the reverse merger of ICICI and three other group entities into ICICI Bank. When I joined, I was the only person in the corporate communications team. Shortly thereafter, a person with extensive institutional knowledge from having been with ICICI for over twenty years joined me. We started as a two-person team and gradually expanded as ICICI launched new businesses, including life and general insurance, credit cards and more.

To give you a brief history of the bank, ICICI itself had been established in 1955 by the World Bank, Indian government and the corporate sector as a development financial institution, focusing on project financing. ICICI Bank, as we know it today, was launched in 1994. I joined the parent ICICI in 2000. By then, ICICI was already listed and had made history by being one of the first Indian companies to issue American depositary receipts (ADR) on the New York Stock Exchange, alongside Infosys.

By mid-2005, I received an offer from Deutsche Bank, and the allure of working with a global organisation as a director was too enticing to pass up, especially at the age of thirty-six. The launch of its retail banking segment enticed me, but by 2007, it became clear that it wouldn't become a major focus, and the bank would continue to concentrate more on its corporate side. It left me longing for a bigger challenge and a broader canvas.

Around that time, Vodafone, which had just entered India by acquiring Hutchison's stake in Hutch Essar, was looking for a head of corporate communications. I decided to join this role in late 2007 and spent around three years there. Then, towards the end of 2010, I transitioned back into banking when I joined Citibank as the head of corporate affairs for South Asia. Just as I joined Citibank, Deutsche Bank reached out and asked me to return. Around that time, Anshu Jain, who has since passed away, was about to become the global co-CEO of Deutsche Bank. That was good enough for me to return and work with them. I rejoined Deutsche Bank at the end of 2011 and stayed there until mid-2015.

By then, I had been leading corporate communications departments in several organisations, and begun to feel that while the brand and work were evolving, the role itself hadn't changed much. I wanted to explore whether I could handle a business on my own. This desire, coupled with a growing sense that I needed something new, led to conversations with Reshma Ghoshal, the head of brand and internal communications at Deutsche Bank, who seemed to share a similar mindset. So, we decided to venture out together.

The challenge then was how to approach Deutsche Bank and tell Mr Jain that I wanted to leave. Well, as it turned out, he stepped down at the end of June, and two days later, I sent an email to my boss expressing my intent to leave. By mid-August, I was out of the company. Reshma and I had agreed to leave in a staggered manner so that there was enough time for a smooth handover. Reshma joined me towards the end of September, and together we launched The Good Edge in September 2015. That marks the beginning of my journey into the PR consulting business.

Reshma handles the creative and content side, while I focus on the media and communications services. In all my corporate communications jobs, we never found a single PR firm that would meet all the company's communication needs. We often required a mix of consultancies—a marketing agency, an advertising agency, a PR consultancy along with content writers and advisory services—to cover our requirements. Additionally, finding firms that could provide strategic advisory to leadership was not easy.

Reshma and I were clear that we wanted our firm to mirror corporate communications as closely as possible. We didn't want to be just a PR firm or content agency; we would be a full-service consultancy capable of providing advisory services and executing all types of communications needs. We used to describe ourselves as a 'corporate communications consultancy' rather than just a PR firm. This vision shaped the way we structured our organisation, with a focus on integrating various services under one roof from the start.

We were intentional about having senior people in leadership positions, which is atypical for a new PR firm. We also made sure that we could offer a wide range of services, including content creation, creative design, research, CSR advisory and communications services. Our goal was always to provide a more comprehensive approach to communications.

The journey has been rewarding, though it started with the usual challenges that any new organisation faces, especially in the services sector. If you don't have an existing client base to rely on, it can take some time to get the business rolling. However, being in a profession you understand and being willing to put in the hard work make a big difference. Mumbai is a generous city where people are willing to give you a chance, even if you're a new business. If you do well, you can build momentum.

Patience was key, and we were advised by several senior professionals to ensure we could support ourselves for at least a year without relying on new business. This advice was extremely helpful. The first few months were slow, with very little business coming in. We reached out to several companies, pitched our services and gradually started getting small projects for content creation, creative work, and events.

Our big break came when K.V. Kamath, who had become the president of BRICS Bank, reached out to us. We set up the bank's new identity and enabled it to launch itself as the newest multilateral development bank with a difference. I spent a couple of months in Shanghai working on the project. It also helped us build credibility and gave us something to show when talking to other potential clients.

After that, things started to pick up in May and June 2016. And then in August 2016 we were fortunate to be brought on board for the launch of Jio. That marked a huge step forward for our firm.

Being an entrepreneur isn't as difficult as it might seem. In many ways, it's similar to working in a corporate environment, as both come with their own stresses. In the corporate world, there's often a lot of politics at play, and you have to navigate that as well. As an entrepreneur, you're responsible for your decisions and their outcomes, but you also have more freedom to make them. If you do good work, people will give you a chance. Once you get that opportunity, it's up to you to prove yourself.

3

Tarun Deo

Founder, Progressive Communications

'...Stay adaptable and keep finding ways to innovate.'

Pioneering Tech PR in India

I was born in Mumbai. My father served as a naval officer, which meant frequent relocations as he was posted across India. While Mumbai remained our home base during my early years—partly because my mother's parents were also based there—my father's postings took us to places like Wellington and Cochin.

I initially attended Bombay Scottish School, following in the footsteps of my mother and her sisters. However, with the frequent transfers, it was decided that my sister and I would attend boarding school. That's how I landed at Sherwood in Nainital, where I spent seven transformative years, from grade six through my twelfth standard graduation.

After Sherwood, I joined Delhi University. By then, my parents had settled in Noida following my father's retirement.

I enrolled at Shri Ram College of Commerce, initially opting for an economics course before switching to a BCom degree. These were exciting times in India—the early 1990s—when the country was on the cusp of an economic transformation. Finance Minister Dr Manmohan Singh spearheaded economic reforms to liberalise India's economy to handle a severe balance of payments crisis, which opened up unprecedented opportunities in business and services.

Fresh out of university, I joined a small tech company called Peutronics, which developed the accounting software Tally. At the time, India's tech scene was largely focused on services, so product-oriented companies like Peutronics were rare. My first job was selling Tally software to brokers at the Delhi Stock Exchange—a task that taught me a lot but didn't align with my aspirations. After six months, I realised I wanted something different.

One day, I came across an ad in a newspaper for a company called Perfect Relations. The ad mentioned the company being in the business of public relations, product launches and information campaigns, which intrigued me. I applied and was invited for an interview at their small basement office in Jangpura. There, I met Dilip Cherian, Bobby Kewalramani and Sunil Khosla, and soon my journey in PR began.

At Perfect Relations, my typical day was a mix of learning and executing. In the mornings, I would accompany Dilip or Bobby to meetings, observing how they handled client relationships and strategy discussions. Afternoons were spent writing press releases, pitching story ideas and preparing for media outreach. Evenings involved physically delivering press releases and pitch notes to media houses like the Press Trust of India or visiting the offices of major newspapers on Bahadur Shah Zafar Marg. This hands-on rigour allowed me to build strong connections with journalists, many of whom I remain in touch with even today, despite being based in Singapore for the last twenty years.

This period was both challenging and rewarding. The economic transformation following India's liberalisation brought a wave of opportunities, with companies like PepsiCo entering the market and tech giants like TCS and Infosys gaining prominence. The burgeoning BPO industry leveraged India's tech talent and cost advantages, leading to the establishment of massive call centres. It was an era of transformation, and being part of it was exhilarating.

The experiences and relationships I built during those formative years laid the foundation for my career, teaching me the importance of adaptability, resilience, and the value of strong professional networks. Looking back, it was the perfect time to begin a career in an India that was rapidly reinventing itself.

Around that time, conversations about mobile phones were gaining momentum, with licences being prepped for telecom giants like BT (British Telecom) and AT&T. Similarly, major tech companies like Microsoft were exploring opportunities to establish R&D centres in India and introduce their products to this rapidly evolving market. It was a period of unparalleled growth and transformation across multiple sectors, each brimming with potential.

This was particularly thrilling for someone like me, who thrives on information. The excitement of tracking new entrants into the Indian market, high-profile leadership changes, groundbreaking product launches or the evolving standards for mobile telephony was unmatched. It felt like being at the epicentre of a knowledge explosion, and I loved every moment of it.

During this era, the nuances of communication strategy became increasingly apparent. Media relations were critical—far more so than they are in today's internet-driven world. Engaging with journalists, shaping messaging, managing corporate reputation, and strategising CSR initiatives were essential. It was an incredible time to be part of India's communications fraternity.

I spent five enriching years at Perfect Relations, working on diverse projects, particularly in the tech space. Then, Text100 came knocking. Known as a tech-specialist PR firm, Text100 had just established itself as the first fully owned foreign PR subsidiary in India. Their entry was anchored by two marquee clients: Microsoft and BT. They were assembling a team to handle these significant market-entry mandates, and I joined their Delhi office to lead the BT account.

BT was deeply immersed in the telecom revolution, bidding for mobile licences and driving the sector forward. It was an intense and exciting account to manage, particularly under the leadership of Arun Seth, who headed BT in India. Text100's Delhi office housed the Microsoft and BT accounts, while their Bangalore office catered to consumer tech-focused clients like Compaq.

As Text100 expanded, the next logical step was opening an office in Mumbai, especially as the dot-com boom took off. Mumbai emerged as the hub for dot-com start-ups, complementing Delhi's focus on public affairs and government relations and Bangalore's tech specialisation.

At the age of twenty-seven, my boss and mentor at Text100, Sandeep Kalsi, entrusted me with the responsibility of setting up the Mumbai office. It was a bold move, as we started with no clients, relying solely on Text100's stellar reputation and the market's explosive potential.

I relocated to Mumbai with my wife, and within a few months we gained tremendous traction. We secured clients like SAP, McKinsey and a host of dot-com companies. Within two years, the Mumbai office became the fastest-growing branch in Text100's network, marking a transformative phase in both my career and the company's growth story.

By the late 1990s, just before the turn of the millennium, I was promoted to MD of Text100 India. This new role brought me back to Delhi in the early 2000s.

As MD of Text100 India, I had the privilege of leading the firm during a transformative period. Our client roster now included industry giants like Microsoft, BT, SAP, Compaq, McKinsey, Canon and Xerox. It was a heady time, full of energy and growth, as the firm gained recognition as a formidable player in the industry.

One of the highlights of that phase was building an incredible team. I was fortunate to hire talented individuals like Zach James, Rishi Seth, and Shafaat Hussain, among others. This young and dynamic team gave Text100 a competitive edge, allowing us to challenge established firms like Adfactors, Perfect Relations and Genesis. Despite being a relatively young firm, our collective hunger and passion for the work set us apart.

That said, I was always mindful of the environment we operated in. The Indian PR business was still nascent, only about seven or eight years old. While we were talented and ambitious, we also benefitted from being in the right place at the right time. The profession's rapid growth created opportunities for everyone—truly a 'rising tide floats all boats' scenario.

By the early 2000s, Text100 India had grown to around eighty people, a remarkable size for a consultancy in India at the time. We were thriving, and I loved the work. However, I started to think about the future of communications in India. While the market was growing, I realised it would take time to reach full maturity. I wanted to accelerate my learning curve by experiencing a more developed and evolved communications landscape.

With that in mind, I floated the idea of exploring opportunities outside India to my boss. I explained that while I was confident I could continue excelling in my current role, stepping into a more advanced market would exponentially enhance my learning and broaden my perspective.

At that time, Text100 had about four or five offices in the Asia Pacific, in addition to three in India. These included Singapore, Hong Kong, China, Japan and Australia. Singapore stood out to me as an ideal destination. It was a true regional hub, with numerous multinational companies headquartered there. While it remains a hub today, its significance two decades ago was even greater.

My boss encouraged me to consider how I could contribute to the Singapore office. I pointed out that while Text100 had a strong presence across Asia, the offices operated somewhat independently. We could build stronger regional cohesion and strategic alignment, which could amplify Text100's impact in the region.

My goal was to establish a strong regional proposition for Text100. By building a network of professionals with multi-market responsibilities, we could position Text100 as a single, cohesive consultancy capable of managing communications across the region. The idea was to offer clients a seamless solution—one consultancy that could handle markets like India, Japan, China and Singapore—eliminating the complexity of coordinating with multiple consultancies across different countries. This approach became one of the first regional propositions crafted in the business.

In 2002, I moved to Singapore. However, shortly after my relocation, Asia faced its first pandemic—the SARS outbreak. It was a challenging time, but it coincided with a remarkable opportunity. Text100 had just won IBM's global business, marking a pivotal moment for the firm. One of the key mandates was managing the divestiture of IBM's Personal Computing Division, which included ThinkPad laptops, desktops and servers, as IBM shifted its focus to becoming a services company.

What made this deal extraordinary was the buyer: Lenovo, a relatively unknown Chinese company at the time, was acquiring an iconic American business line, with its largest manufacturing operations based in Japan. Today, the narrative of Chinese brands going global is familiar, but twenty years ago this was groundbreaking. I had the privilege of being part of one of the earliest such mandates, managing communications for a complex, high-profile transaction that spanned multiple regions.

This opportunity also brought me into close collaboration with Geri Kan, an executive whom IBM had moved from New York to Singapore to lead this project. We often laughed about the succinct mandate her boss gave her: 'Don't F this up.' My own boss gave me the same directive. Together, we navigated the complexities of this landmark deal post the turbulent SARS period.

Managing this project proved to be a strong proof point for our regional proposition. With core strategies being developed in Singapore and implemented across Asia, it showcased Text100's ability to lead and coordinate large-scale, multi-market communications efforts. Once the Lenovo–IBM transaction stabilised, I leveraged this case study to pitch the regional model to clients like Nokia and Cisco, gaining significant traction.

At that time, the Singapore office had just three or four people. But the Lenovo–IBM mandate enabled me to attract top talent from across Asia to build a diverse, high-performing team. We brought in Matt from the US, Blair from Australia, Shafaat from India, and others who brought deep expertise from various markets. This diverse team became a key strength in demonstrating our regional capabilities.

Thanks to the success of the regional proposition, Text100 opened offices in Malaysia and other South East Asian markets, and existing offices across the region began expanding rapidly. I spent about five years in Singapore, during which time the consultancy solidified its regional footprint and reputation.

In 2007, another opportunity came my way through Bob Winslow, a mentor and former colleague from Text100. Bob had joined FleishmanHillard in the US, where he was tasked with enhancing the consultancy's global tech and digital capabilities. He reached out with an enticing role: heading FleishmanHillard's tech practice in Asia, based out of Hong Kong, while also leading the Asia-Pacific side of AT&T's communications—a cornerstone client for the firm.

The role excited me because it expanded my experience beyond India and South East Asia into North Asia. Hong Kong was buzzing in 2007, with a thriving business environment and the Beijing Olympics on the horizon. My wife and I, with no kids at the time, embraced the adventure and moved to Hong Kong. It was an incredible new chapter in both my career and personal life.

I joined FleishmanHillard as their head of digital and tech for APAC, and became the primary advocate for

AT&T. At that time, the AT&T account was worth nearly US$70 million, a huge sum even by today's standards. My journey in Hong Kong began with this pivotal role, and I applied the same approach as before, but this time with a focus on North Asia, and more broadly, the whole of Asia. FleishmanHillard was more established than Text100, and the internet was starting to emerge as a new platform for communication—beyond traditional media to digital and social media channels.

In my role, I continued consulting and building the tech team. But being in charge of digital also put me at the forefront of the profession's evolution, especially in terms of the internet and digital strategies. Until then, PR had followed a pretty standard playbook—press releases, press conferences, product launches, internal communications—executed across cities like Delhi, Mumbai, Kuala Lumpur and Manila. But now, digital was introducing a whole new set of opportunities and challenges.

It was an exciting time, as I worked closely with FleishmanHillard's Washington DC office, which was leading the charge on digital innovation. I made monthly trips to DC, learning firsthand from the experts there. It was a defining time for both the company and the PR profession as a whole.

I spent five years with FleishmanHillard, first in Hong Kong, and then back to Singapore in 2009, due to some operational challenges. The role was expanded to include addressing issues across these offices, as well as in India, which added complexity to the job.

By 2011–2012, after spending over a decade in seven cities across six countries, I decided to take a break. My wife and I had just adopted a daughter, and I wanted to focus on enjoying that precious time with her—picking her up from play school, having lunch together, and simply being present. I took about six to nine months off, but soon realised I was ready for the next challenge.

That's when Golin came calling. I had a great conversation with Jon Hughes, who had been sent to Hong Kong to streamline Golin's operations in Asia. John introduced me to Fred Cook, the CEO of Golin, and after two engaging conversations with them, I was offered the role of head of Golin's Singapore office. While this wasn't a regional role per se, it involved leading the South East Asia office, which, at that time, was a small team of ten to twelve people.

By this point, the digital landscape had completely exploded. It was clear that no consultancy could continue operating in the old PR model, focusing only on media relations. Digital strategy had to be a core component of any PR firm's offering, even if it wasn't fully defined yet. Golin was looking for someone who could lead this transition, and that was exactly what drew me to the role.

Singapore had limited media, which meant we had to explore digital solutions. I wasn't sure if I had fully cracked the code yet, but I was eager to give it a try. This is where my journey at Golin began.

Soon, it became clear that if we wanted to have a meaningful online presence and advise clients on their digital footprint, we needed to rethink how we operated. PR firms traditionally focused on the written word, but with digital it was crucial to think beyond that—creativity, technology, and new skill sets were all essential. That's when we took a bold step and created a creative team at Golin called DAC—Digital Analytics and Content. This team wasn't just a support function but a profit centre in its own right; it was vital to monetise the digital capabilities we were developing. If we didn't, how could we attract the right talent or justify the investment in specialised skills?

A great ally in this journey was Shouvik Mukherjee, whom I promoted to creative director. Together, we cracked the digital, analytics and content code. We became one of the first PR consultancies to deliver films and run influencer relations programmes, which was incredibly exciting. While the traditional media side of the business continued, building DAC was a game-changer.

During my seven years at Golin, this approach helped transform the Singapore office from a small team to a much larger, more dynamic firm. Then came COVID-19, which impacted everyone. The changes at Golin were significant, too—Fred Cook, the CEO, had moved on, and we had a three-CEO structure that was, depending on whom you asked, either working well or very confusing. One day, I got a call from Jon, my boss, to join a meeting where I was told that he was leaving. At that point, I started reflecting on my future, especially after being at Golin for eight years and hitting the age of fifty.

I decided that instead of joining another company, it was time to venture out on my own. And that's how Progressive came into being. It's been three-and-a-half years since, and it hasn't been easy. The world is in a very different place now, with new challenges, from competition and geopolitical issues to changes in client needs. But I'm optimistic. We're a small, nimble firm with a team of just seven or eight people, which allows us to be agile and spot new opportunities. We focus on being a micro-agency with big capabilities, rather than expanding into multiple offices like in the past.

To navigate this, we've formed some great partnerships: The Shed 28 in Singapore, Peppercomm (a Ruder Finn company) for North America and China access, Simply Thought for data analytics and measurement, First Partners in India, Access Communications in Korea, and Rantau in Malaysia. These partnerships allow us to offer full-service solutions, leveraging my experience and the networks I've built over the years. My clients know that, by working with me, they're getting access to a high level of expertise, just like they would with larger firms.

Starting a firm is never easy, but the challenges are the same whether you're in India or elsewhere. While markets like India, China and the US are massive and have their own complexities, places like Singapore, Malaysia, Indonesia or Germany present their own unique set of challenges. However, regardless of the location, the key is to stay adaptable and keep finding ways to innovate.

Emergence of Social Media Platforms

Over the last two decades, public relations has undergone a remarkable evolution, driven by technological advancements, changing consumer behaviours and the growing integration of digital and social media platforms. The transformation has redefined the strategies, tools and expectations surrounding how organisations communicate with their audiences and manage their reputations.

In the early 2000s, PR was heavily reliant on traditional media. We focused on securing coverage in newspapers, magazines, television and radio to shape public perception. Press releases, media kits, and personal relationships with journalists were the core tools of the trade. Campaigns were often evaluated based on media coverage metrics such as circulation and audience reach.

Crisis communication during this period revolved around swift responses through established media outlets. Social listening was limited, as most consumer feedback came through letters, calls or surveys. The role of PR professionals was clear: act as intermediaries between clients and the press.

In the mid-2000s, the rise of the internet began to shift the PR landscape dramatically. Online news platforms and blogs emerged as influential voices. Simultaneously, websites and email newsletters became essential for organisations to communicate directly with stakeholders.

Search engine optimisation (SEO) and digital content strategy started gaining traction as PR practitioners recognised the importance of online visibility. A successful PR campaign was no longer solely about media hits; it also considered how well an organisation could be found online.

The emergence of social media platforms like Facebook, X (earlier Twitter) and Instagram was arguably the most significant catalyst for change in PR. These platforms enabled two-way communication between organisations and their audiences and democratised the dissemination of information. Suddenly, PR professionals had the opportunity—and the challenge—of engaging directly with consumers.

Social media also amplified the speed and scope of crisis communication. A single negative tweet could spark widespread backlash, requiring organisations to monitor and respond in real time. PR professionals began integrating social media management and analytics into their strategies, leveraging tools like Hootsuite to track conversations and measure impact.

By the 2010s, content marketing and PR became increasingly intertwined. Organisations started to see the value of telling their own stories through blogs, videos, podcasts and other owned media channels. Influencer marketing also emerged as a powerful tactic, with PR campaigns leveraging partnerships with bloggers, YouTubers and social media personalities to reach niche audiences. Campaign metrics shifted from traditional media impressions to digital engagement, such as likes, shares, comments and website traffic. The ability to track campaigns with precision made PR more accountable and data-driven.

Today, PR is a highly integrated discipline, blending traditional strategies with digital innovations. Media monitoring, sentiment analysis and even content generation are now done with the assistance of AI and machine learning. VR and AR are also making their way into experiential PR campaigns.

The rise of ESG (environmental, social and governance) considerations has also influenced PR, as organisations are increasingly expected to demonstrate social responsibility and transparency. Stakeholder engagement now includes conscious consumers, activists, policymakers and employees.

In summary, PR over the last twenty years has evolved from a primarily reactive, media-centric practice to a proactive, multi-channel and technology-driven discipline. As the digital landscape continues to evolve, so too will the strategies and tools of PR professionals, ensuring the field remains dynamic and relevant.

4

Nikhil Dey

Executive Director, Adfactors PR

'...I don't fit into a conventional box, and I'm perfectly comfortable with that.'

Weekday Consultant to a Weekend Coach

I was born in Chennai, but my parents worked in the Nilgiris on a tea plantation. I enjoyed the plantation life in the Blue Hills—lovely big bungalows, manicured lawns, gardens and open spaces, camping, fishing trips and plenty of dogs is what home was all about.

I stayed on the estate with my parents, but when it came to my education, there were only two options: boarding school or living with my grandparents in Chennai. My grandparents kindly took me in, and from first to seventh standard, I lived with them.

My paternal grandparents played a huge role in shaping my formative years. They doted on me, pampered me and gave me a childhood filled with love and indulgence. But this blissful period came to an end when my grandfather suffered a heart attack and could no longer manage looking after us.

From seventh to twelfth standard, my younger sister Nisha, four years my junior, and I were sent to boarding school in Ooty—St George's Homes in Ketti Valley, also called the Laidlaw Memorial School. The pampered life I had enjoyed was in stark contrast with the regimented boarding school environment. It was a tough but transformative phase in my life.

Boarding school taught me self-reliance and resilience. I also had to take care of Nisha. The school emphasised holistic development—you had to study rigorously and participate in every sport, whether you were good at it or not. From cricket to hockey, football to gymnastics, tennis to boxing, I had to try it all.

One of the defining moments of my boarding school years happened in the eleventh standard when I got caught drinking with some friends. Ironically, I'm allergic to alcohol and turn bright red after just a sip! Back then, I didn't know that, and a group of us decided to try it out. We were caught, publicly caned and suspended.

Suspension during Easter holidays meant solitary confinement in the dormitory while everyone else went home. We were literally locked in, with food passed to us through window bars. Looking back, it's almost comical, but at the time, it was a deeply traumatic experience.

Yet, this two-week punishment was a turning point. With nothing else to do, I began studying seriously for the first time in my life. From being near the bottom of my class, I shot up to second place, discovering for the first time potential I hadn't tapped into.

That incident taught me an important life lesson: once you realise you're capable of something, the only thing that can stop you is yourself. From that moment on, my academic performance improved dramatically.

Another lasting memory from that episode was how my parents handled it. When my father came to pick me up, he had no idea what had happened—the principal's letter informing him of my suspension hadn't arrived yet. Dad had brought along a video camera to record my school play, but he must have sensed something in my demeanour and put the camera away.

When I explained the situation, I was bracing myself for anger. Instead, he said, 'Nikhil, I'm very disappointed in you.' I immediately apologised, feeling terrible, but then he added, 'Not because you drank, you stupid bugger—do what you want, but don't get caught! Be smarter than that. You're my son!'

That response was so unexpected that it completely disarmed me. My parents normalised the mistake and focused on how I could learn from it rather than dwelling on the wrongdoing itself. Their support and light-hearted approach helped me bounce back stronger.

This philosophy—that mistakes are okay as long as you learn from them—has influenced my leadership style. I support people, help them figure out their own answers and encourage them to grow. Whether in my personal life or in my current work as a coach, I focus on creating a safe environment where mistakes are viewed as opportunities for growth.

Those early experiences taught me resilience, the value of hard work and the importance of unwavering support in helping others thrive.

I spent five years at Loyola College in Chennai. After completing my BA in economics, I was confident when I wrote the CAT exam—maybe too confident. I was convinced I'd get into an IIM on my first attempt. When I didn't make it, I decided to continue with my master's degree as a fallback.

The second time I attempted, I was more prepared and applied to multiple institutes. That's how I ended up at the International Management Institute (IMI) in New Delhi. I used to joke about aiming for IIM but landing at IMI. Nevertheless, this turn of events set the stage for my journey into PR.

During my MBA, I discovered a love for marketing, advertising and communication. Courses like 'Advertising and Communications Management' and 'Written and Oral Communication' fascinated me. Coincidentally, the latter was taught by Dilip Cherian, who founded Perfect Relations. When final placements came around, I was keen on marketing roles. Ashwani Singla, a senior from the previous batch, had joined a firm called Clea PR and returned for placements. I applied for a role at Clea, was offered a job and had to make a pivotal decision.

This was 1996, the early days of PR in India. Back then, PR wasn't well understood, and many questioned my choice to join the field after an MBA. Some even mocked it, saying PR didn't require professional qualifications. But I saw a chance to make a mark in a growing profession. I felt that being a big fish in a small pond made sense, especially as PR firms weren't targeting MBA graduates like advertising and marketing companies were. Additionally, Clea's offer allowed me to return to Chennai and set up their new office. It felt like a dream—heading an office and opening a new market right after B-school.

However, upon reaching Chennai, I learnt that Clea's plan to open the Chennai office had been deferred. Instead, I was asked to report to Mumbai. Moving to Mumbai on a starting salary of ₹8,000 felt impossible, given the city's costs. After I explained my predicament to Ashwani, he negotiated a solution: Clea would cover my accommodation for the first year. With that, I packed my bags and headed to Mumbai, determined to build a career in PR.

Starting out in PR was both challenging and exhilarating. I joined Clea, as a trainee and left five years later as the branch head of the Delhi office. In those early days, Clea was a dynamic firm, handling high-profile clients like Coca-Cola and major events like the Michael Jackson concert and the Channel [V] Music Awards.

My journey within Clea was marked by pivotal moments. One such moment came when my first boss, Sabiana Anandaraj, announced she was leaving, entrusting me to handle a major client. This was just two years into my career, and I saw an opportunity. I approached the client directly, proposing that I lead the account instead of hiring someone senior. They agreed, and I gained my first portfolio of clients.

Another turning point was being seconded to Channel [V] as an in-house publicity manager when their communications lead went on maternity leave. Despite my limited experience, I was managing high-stakes PR at a time when Channel [V] was competing fiercely with MTV. It was here that I realised the transformative power of PR.

At Channel [V], I developed a framework called the NITWIT principle—an acronym for 'Nonconformist, Irreverent, Trendsetting, Wild, Wacky, Innovative and Topical'. I used NITWIT to drive internal behaviour changes, ensuring that any PR-worthy activity aligned with these attributes. This approach not only improved the raw material for PR but also influenced hiring and programming decisions, making Channel [V] cooler and more competitive.

These early experiences cemented my passion for PR. I loved consultancy life and thrived on the fast-paced environment. Later, my time in corporate communications taught me invaluable lessons about understanding internal organisational dynamics, enhancing my ability to serve clients effectively. Those formative years in PR taught me not just to communicate but to drive meaningful action.

I experienced success very early in my career, which gave me a lot of confidence in my abilities—perhaps even overconfidence at times. About a year later into my work life, I handled the Channel [V] Music Awards, featuring the Spice Girls, and the event was a great success. My boss, marketing head Sunita Rajan, was thrilled with my work.

The first time I met Sunita, I walked into her office dressed in our firm's corporate attire—tie, jacket, the works. She looked at me and said, 'Dude, you're in the wrong place. Lose the jacket, lose the tie. And if you could grow a ponytail, you should. You need to represent Channel [V], and you don't look anything like it.' That was a wake-up call! I embraced a new 'cool' look—jeans and casuals—through the week. But every Friday, when I went back to my office for our meetings, I switched back to the formal suit-and-tie. It was like living a double life!

Around this time, my colleague Ashwani, who was heading our Delhi office, quit and joined Genesis. I wanted a transfer to Bangalore, but Ashwani's resignation meant I was being sent to the Delhi office instead. My boss tore up my transfer letter and said, "You're not going to Bangalore; you're going to Delhi.

I protested, but my boss insisted. Sensing an opportunity, I negotiated a raise from ₹8,000 to ₹11,000 and asked to be made head of the Delhi office. While my boss laughed at first, he ultimately devised a unique solution. He came with me to Delhi, gathered the team and announced a shared leadership model. Three of us—Shobha Soman, Arpana Ahuja and I—would jointly lead the office for a year, after which the team would vote on who would be the head.

It was an unusual arrangement, but a year later, Shobha had decided she did not want the headache of leading an office, and Arpana had joined a client organisation. I was the last one standing. Just four years into my career, I found myself heading a branch office. I built the team, grew the client base and laid a strong foundation for the office. Many of the people I hired, like Santanu Gogoi, Atul Sharma, Atipriya Sarawat, Pooja Garg and Sitara Achreja, are still my close friends today.

Those days were challenging. I barely spoke Hindi, had no connections in Delhi and was competing against stalwarts like Dilip Cherian and Prema Sagar. Things weren't going the way I thought they would for the head of a city office. Pitches were happening everywhere, but I wasn't even being invited. Our office was downsized, and I had to think creatively to make an impact.

That's when inspiration struck. I bought 200 potted plants and got handmade cards with eco-friendly jute strings. On one side, I wrote 'Ideas are meant to grow.' And on the other, I handwrote my mobile number. I created a list of 200 dream clients and instructed my team to deliver the plants personally—not to receptionists or assistants, but directly to the decision-makers. It didn't matter how they managed it—whether they intercepted someone in the parking lot or on the staircase—but the plant had to be handed over directly.

Within weeks, my phone started ringing. The plants sparked curiosity—there was no branding, just the plant and my number. This strategy was a game changer. From being excluded from pitches, we suddenly became a contender—and soon started winning. I learnt that with creativity, resilience and a determined team, you can turn things around, even with limited resources. It was a pivotal point, not just for the office but for my confidence and leadership journey.

One of the breakthrough moments during this period was winning the *Encyclopaedia Britannica* account, which was special because I secured it against stiff competition from Genesis. Interestingly, I later learnt this win caught the attention of Prema Sagar, who had founded Genesis and had no idea who I was until then. She later admitted it was the moment she decided she wanted me on her team.

At the time, though, resources were limited. The office had just one shared desktop, and I had to rent a laptop every time I prepared for pitches. To save costs, I'd plan three pitches on the same day. But then came the CNBC Asia pitch, and something went awry—I didn't have access to a laptop. With no petty cash and no budget, I decided to improvise.

I called my driver Justin, who was my trusted companion and happened to speak Tamil, making communication seamless. I asked him to unplug our office desktop, including the monitor, and load it into the backseat of my Maruti 800. Suit and tie on, I carried the CPU while Justin carried the monitor into Raghav Bahl's office. I set it up right on the conference table and gave my pitch. To Raghav's credit, he didn't bat an eyelid at the unusual set-up. I won the account, which turned into a significant retainer business.

That win taught me a valuable lesson: it's not about the resources you lack but about your ability to make things happen with what you have. Every time I hear complaints about a sticky laptop key or minor inconveniences these days, I think back to those days of hustle. It's a reminder to focus on what you *can* do and to act.

I also learnt the importance of resilience and backing yourself. Both Vinod Nair, Clea's MD, and Ashwani gave me the freedom to experiment and fail, which allowed me to grow tremendously.

This wonderful world of PR gave me my wife Deepa, whom I met at Clea and got married to after a whirlwind six-month romance. She continues to be my best friend, philosopher, critic and best wisher as we come up on the twenty-five-year milestone in 2025.

As my career progressed, so did life's responsibilities. After marriage, financial concerns started weighing on me. Though I had perks like a company car and accommodation, my salary remained low, which was worrisome because we were about to welcome our first child. Out of the blue, a headhunter reached out regarding a role heading the communications team at Fiat India. Initially, I wasn't interested—I loved my job, my team and the life I had built. But Deepa convinced me to attend the interview, saying there was no harm in exploring.

I approached the interview casually, which, ironically, worked in my favour. I breezed through rounds with HR, marketing and even the CEO. When they made an offer, I panicked—I didn't want to leave my current role. To deter them, I made an outrageous counteroffer: a vice president title and three times the salary. To my surprise, they came back a few months later agreeing to all my demands.

That's how, with just five-and-a-half years of PR experience, I became the vice president of corporate communications at Fiat India. The role was a huge leap in terms of responsibility and learning. There weren't any '30 under 30' or '40 under 40' lists then, but the milestones I achieved during my mid-twenties felt like they would've qualified. It was a whirlwind period of growth and opportunity—one I'll always cherish.

Transitioning from consultancy to the role of head of communications at Fiat India was an exciting shift, but over time I realised something was missing. I missed the process of building and coaching teams—an aspect that was integral to my consultancy roles but less prominent in the corporate set-up.

At Fiat, I worked with a small team—my senior colleague, Marius, and me, along with a PR firm I eventually onboarded. This limited scope for team building and nurturing. Nonetheless, I gained a deep understanding of crisis communication and became an active agent of change within the organisation.

One of the most significant challenges Fiat faced then was its poor service reputation—great cars but a subpar service experience. This perception had to be tackled at its root, not just through superficial PR campaigns. Initially, I met resistance from the service head, who told me bluntly to 'stick to PR and leave service to the experts'. Undeterred, I worked on building rapport and eventually collaborated with the team to drive impactful changes.

We introduced a new service policy that enabled proactive follow-ups with customers, addressing a glaring gap in the customer journey. I also worked closely with the service team to improve Fiat's JD Power rankings. A year of focused effort paid off, earning Fiat recognition as the 'most improved brand' in service—an achievement rooted in meaningful change, not just spin.

This period taught me the immense value of integrating communication strategies with business objectives. PR isn't just about storytelling; it's about solving real problems and then telling those stories.

As I missed the dynamic, team-centric environment of consultancy life, I began conducting weekend training sessions for Hanmer & Partners, designing a year-long programme to upskill their teams. These interactions opened the door to my return to the consultancy world.

Both Hanmer and Genesis approached me with offers—Hanmer as CEO and Genesis as head of Delhi. The Hanmer offer was tempting; becoming a CEO before the age of thirty was a dream. I took a step back to evaluate where I would grow the most. Genesis, with its global affiliation as Genesis Burson-Marsteller, larger client portfolio and the scale of its Delhi operations, presented a richer opportunity, even if the title wasn't as grand.

Choosing Genesis required me to prioritise long-term learning over short-term optics. That choice set the stage for a fifteen-year journey, where I eventually became the president of both PR and public affairs.

Some of the clients that I had the opportunity to partner with were PepsiCo India, Indigo and Royal Enfield. A crisis, and two brands that taught me so much, offer just a peep into the journey. There was a big takeaway from the PepsiCo pesticide crisis. When peacetime finally came, PepsiCo used it well. They invested in an exercise where I travelled to all their plants and regional offices across the country and ran crisis preparedness workshops. It is the hallmark of a good company that it learns from difficult experiences and builds best practices. In subsequent years, PepsiCo responded to several issues with speed and ownership.

Indigo, from the first launch press event, till my last day at Burson, was another client I had many occasions to support.

I travelled with Indigo from traditional PR into the world of digital and beyond. Aligning our crisis and issues response with their central operations team was a great way to ensure we were able to navigate the 24/7 demands of the aviation industry in a social media world. Royal Enfield, from the days when Siddharth Lal was based in India and attending monthly PR review meetings till now, where I work with the Eicher Foundation to give shape to the messaging related to their social mission, has been one of my longest relationships. Both these brands stand out as great examples of clear messaging: 'On time, low cost and hassle-free' for Indigo and 'Pure Motorcycling' for Royal Enfield, which has resulted in a differentiated reputation messaging. I built my credentials as a media trainer and conductor of messaging and crisis preparedness workshops at these brands.

In the midst of the COVID-19 pandemic, I explored new opportunities. After years at Genesis, I had a brief stint with another firm but soon realised I was again at a crossroads, searching for a role that aligned with my evolving priorities. During this time, I engaged in discussions with two global firms. Simultaneously, I reconnected with Madan Bahal, someone I had been speaking with over the years.

The process with Madan was unique—seven or eight rounds of Sunday talks conducted remotely due to the pandemic. These discussions eventually clarified what I wanted next. By then, I had reached a new level of self-awareness, shaped by my coaching journey. I became a certified coach in 2019 and achieved accreditation in 2021. This 'inside-out' journey helped me identify what was most important to me: meaningful work and the ability to balance my professional and personal aspirations.

Adfactors PR stood out among my opportunities, not just for its scale and entrepreneurial culture but also because it allowed me to pursue coaching alongside my communications work. Few organisations would enable this, but Adfactors not only supported my weekend coaching practice but also encouraged me to bring it into their ecosystem. Today, I proudly call myself a weekday communicator and weekend coach, a dual role that feels incredibly fulfilling.

Adfactors PR provided the perfect canvas for me at this stage in my career. It combined the entrepreneurial mindset I had cultivated early in my journey with the institutional approach I honed in global firms and corporate roles. The firm's readiness to gear up for the demands of the twenty-first century resonated with my vision, creating a partnership that felt almost serendipitous.

Now, nearly five years into my Adfactors PR journey, I find myself balancing the tasks of building teams, shaping strategies and fostering innovation in an environment that demands creativity and entrepreneurial thinking. It feels like the culmination of everything I've learnt so far—an intersection of passion, purpose, and possibility.

Five years in Clea, fifteen years with Genesis BM (now Burson), a few with Weber Shandwick, and the last half-decade with India's largest PR firm, Adfactors PR, make for nearly twenty-eight years in this profession. I have had the privilege of working with and for many wonderful people, brands and companies.

One of the lessons that I learnt in my formative years in this profession was the need to have a signature style. To stand out from the crowd, one needs to be different or do different. This was taught to me by a then-colleague and now friend, Rajesh

Dube. I remember an incident when I was sitting behind a press registration desk at a hotel during an assignment, feeling rather sorry for myself. When Rajesh came up to me, I launched into a tirade about how I had not studied so much to spend my time handing out press kits and collecting visiting cards. That was the first time Rajesh told me about leaving my signature style on projects. I asked him with sarcasm how I was supposed to leave my 'Special Dey fingerprints' on a press desk. Without saying another word, Rajesh showed me. The desk had a bunch of notepads and some pencils strewn next to them. Two cardboard boxes behind me contained the press kits and some media giveaways. Dubes, as he is fondly called by friends, got a tablecloth, covered the desk and pushed the cardboard boxes out of sight. Pencils were sharpened and put in two glasses, the pads were arranged neatly and a flower vase added some colour and character to the desk. A bowl with a sign saying 'Please drop your card here' appeared. And just like that, the press registration desk was transformed. Now whenever I feel that the job is boring or beneath me, I ask myself, 'How can I make the ordinary extraordinary?' It is also a reminder that no assignment is too big or too small; if I am at the table, I will make it matter, and always try and add a touch of Dey to it.

One of the things I'm extremely proud of is my contribution to talent development in the profession. I'm currently the chair of the Public Relations Consultants Association of India's (PRCAI) Academia and Talent Development. We recently launched our first elective course in reputation management at IIM Udaipur. But my involvement in teaching goes back to the early 1990s. I've taught at various institutes, and I truly enjoy spending time with young minds on campuses.

Over the last five years, my professional life has evolved and I am now a leadership and life coach. I am an International Coaching Federation (ICF)-accredited coach and the first winner of the Rising Star of the Coaching Industry in India award. My coaching practice is called soul2sole coaching, and it is all about aligning the inner you (the soul) with the outer journey (your sole), and where your footsteps lead you. This inner and other alignment also mirrors the work I do in the world of PR, by getting brands to identify their true north and stay on message.

What makes me unique is that I don't fit into a conventional box, and I'm perfectly comfortable with that. It takes both the right organisation and the right individual to embrace this approach. For me to feel at ease in this space is a skill in itself. While many people may question their identity or struggle with labels, I focus on delivering value in the present. As long as I'm making an impact this week, I'm content. I'll let life unfold and see where it takes me next. That is the essence of enjoying the journey.

New Rules, New Tools, Same Game

The way I explain the evolution of PR from the time I got into the business till now is 'new rules, new tools, same game'. At its core, the profession remains rooted in being the custodian of reputation. No other function is tasked with building and maintaining regular engagement with all stakeholders. The world is moving into the zone of instant gratification and goldfish attention spans. New rules and new tools come into play when you have to build meaningful two-way dialogue and relationships in this always-on world. YouTube influencers and podcasters today are where attention is earned and sometimes paid for.

My favourite definition of public relations is: 'PR is doing good and then getting credit for it.' I love this definition because it places equal emphasis on being the author of action as well as the amplifier of the message and the last-mile communicator. Too often in PR, ideation and actions are planned and executed by others and then the PR team is called in for the last-mile communications. There is much value in being able to create publicity, but there is even more when you can get a company to act by virtue of curating big bold ideas and then getting them talked about.

On this front, in some cases, we have gone a few steps back. In the early years, there was more freedom to experiment and try new things. Now there is a more formulaic approach and boundaries have been placed around the PR team. Breaking free of these as the lines between advertising, marketing, digital, experiential and PR all blur is a big opportunity, if one has the courage and energy to grasp it. One of the roles I have the opportunity of playing at Adfactors is to lead the Centre of Excellence. All the contemporary capabilities that we are building from social impact and ESG consulting, to video storytelling, thought leadership, analytics and digital reputation management, are tools that enable us to navigate critical issues on behalf of clients and play the same PR game in a way that works in today's context.

5

Deepshikha Dharmaraj

CEO, Burson Group, India

'Doing the right thing, knowing when to say no, and focusing on what truly matters ...'

One Company—Three Decades and Counting

I was born in 1972 in the air force base in Bareilly, Uttar Pradesh. My father was with the Indian Air Force and both grandparents were also in the armed forces, so I grew up as a typical 'fauji kid'.

Unfortunately, I lost both my parents when I was four years old, so most of my childhood was spent with my grandparents. My grandmother, in particular, played a significant role in raising me and my younger sister. One of the key lessons she instilled in us was the importance of values—doing the right thing, knowing when to say no and focusing on what truly matters, especially when it's about family and friends. These lessons have stayed with me throughout my life, and I hope I've been able to pass them on to my child.

Unfortunately, we lost our grandmother when I was sixteen. After that, my aunt, whom I later came to call my mother, Akash Dharmaraj, took on the responsibility of raising us. She, too, played a significant role in making me who I am today. She instilled in me the importance of independence and resilience.

My life has been shaped by three incredibly strong women: my grandmother, Akash and Prema Sagar, who became my mentor. They taught me to stand on my feet, to be strong as a woman, ready to take risks and to not depend on others for support. I have followed these guiding principles in both my personal and professional life.

I went to Air Force Bal Bharti in Delhi, where I studied from grade one to grade twelve. The stability of being in one school for so long gave me a solid foundation, and even today, I remain close to the friends I made back then.

After school, I initially wanted to pursue architecture but ended up enrolling in an economics honours degree at Miranda House. Surprisingly, I enjoyed it. It was a bit of a shift from my science background in school, but a newfound love for maths took me to a master's degree in business economics, which focused on applying econometrics in business. Here, I majored in marketing. But while I experimented with marketing assignments, something just didn't click, and I started rethinking the direction I wanted to take. That's when I reconnected with Prema, who had just set up Genesis PR. She was a family friend, but I never knew much about her profession.

As I was talking to her about my uncertainty regarding a career in marketing, she quickly suggested that I join Genesis. I remember being puzzled and asking, 'What is Genesis? And what exactly is public relations?' My master's programme had only dedicated two short paragraphs to PR, describing it vaguely as managing relationships with stakeholders and dealing with the media. I had no idea what the field actually involved.

Prema had just completed a course with Frank Jefkins in the UK then and started the firm, which had employed four people—Archana Jain, Nandita Lakshmanan, Geeta Singh and Sulakshana Pathak. I would be the fifth person in the team. I decided to give it a shot for six months, thinking that if it didn't work out I could always find another job. Prema agreed, and I was on board.

Well, six months turned into thirty years. We were a small firm back then, but the excitement of building something new kept me engaged and motivated from day one.

Every day at Genesis brought something new—whether it was a new client or a fresh challenge. People often ask me how I stayed in one company for so long. But when I share what I've accomplished during that time, it becomes clear: I was able to reinvent my role every five years. Each stage of the company's growth offered me chances to take on new responsibilities, which kept me engaged and motivated.

Genesis has taught me a lot, especially about leadership. I've always strived to do something new and different. I have adapted well to constant change. Back then, we didn't call it having a 'growth mindset', but that's what I've always had. It's about not viewing problems as obstacles but as opportunities. Instead of complaining about issues, I've always asked, 'How can we solve this? How can we do better?'

Even as a child, I wasn't interested in competing with classmates for better grades. It was more about personal improvement—how could *I* do better? This mindset has stuck with me over the years. I have rarely compared myself to others but have instead held myself to my own standards. There are moments when I have felt that I haven't done enough, but focusing on improving myself made sure it didn't pull me down.

As a CEO now, I've realised that 80 per cent of the battle is about how you approach your role and the mindset you bring to the office every day. You might be woken up at six in the morning with an urgent situation, and how you choose to react can either make or break it. This mindset is rooted in self-awareness—being conscious of your behaviour, your actions and how they affect the people around you.

My mother, Akash, instilled in me this idea of self-awareness. She was a psychologist and life coach and encouraged my sister and me to be introspective, understand our thoughts and emotions and approach problems with a solution-oriented mindset. During my early years at Genesis in Delhi, I could always lean on her wisdom, and she constantly reminded me of the importance of understanding how our behaviour impacts the people around us—especially in the workplace. Instead of dwelling on what wasn't working, she taught us to think, 'How can we make it work?' That lesson has been a cornerstone of how I've approached both my personal and professional life.

In the first two years at Genesis in Delhi, I witnessed the company grow from a five-person firm to a team of around twenty by the time I moved to Mumbai. Those were exciting times, filled with some very memorable campaigns. One of our biggest clients back then was DCM Daewoo Cielo, and I was fortunate to be the lead of the team that launched India's first mid-size car. At the time, Maruti ruled the small-car industry along with legacy cars like Premier Padmini, Ambassador, and a few international luxury models. Cielo was a game changer, and the buzz we created around its launch became a case study on how to introduce a new vehicle segment to India.

Discovery Channel, which was launching in India, was another fascinating client. There, I had the privilege of working closely with Kiran Karnik, who later became the president of NASSCOM. He was working with ISRO then and brought so much knowledge and perspective to the table. Together, we crafted the strategies to introduce a new category called 'infotainment' to the Indian market. We focused on making Discovery Channel's 'English documentary style' programming appeal to an Indian viewership, which was a unique challenge at the time.

When I moved to Mumbai to start the Genesis office there, I was just twenty-four years old. I still marvel at Prema's trust in me. Being a young woman in a male-dominated profession was tough. I distinctly remember my first pitch to JM Financial Securities in a room full of older men. They looked at me and must have wondered if I was too young to lead the account. But Prema backed me, telling them, 'Don't judge her by her age but by her work.' And she was right—we won over that client and went on to do fantastic work with them. The main client contact from that meeting is still a friend today.

Starting a new office has its own obstacles, but we were a close-knit team and always supported each other. In those early days, I always wore saris to look older and more professional, as wearing dresses or pants made me look like a college student. But it worked, and we built lasting relationships with clients.

Some of the best work of my career happened in those eleven years heading the Mumbai office. We opened a Pune office during that time, and I got to be a part of significant moments in India's telecommunications journey, such as working with

Max Touch, which later became Hutch, Orange and eventually Vodafone. That relationship lasted for a long time.

Another highlight was our work with Hindustan Unilever's beauty brand, Lakmé. We signed up HUL two years after setting up the Mumbai office, even though we were a ten-person team. I remember the head of communications at Unilever at that time asking Prema, 'Who's going to manage our account? Deepshikha might need someone senior.' Prema assured him, saying, 'You can always reach out to me, but give Deepshikha a few months. And then if you feel you need someone senior, we'll revisit this conversation.' That day never came, and we managed PR for the entire HUL portfolio for several years.

In many ways, the FMCG PR landscape in India really took shape from our work at that time. We set the foundation for how consumer brands should approach PR in the country, and who better to learn from than HUL! They are known for producing some of the world's best marketers, so working alongside them was an invaluable experience. We got to collaborate with brilliant minds and laid down the blueprint for how to engage with consumer audiences through PR—understanding what drives them and how PR can effectively connect with them.

One of the most iconic campaigns we worked on was for Lakmé, which was considered 'my mother's brand'—a brand for an older generation. The challenge was to rebrand it and make it appealing to a younger audience. I vividly remember brainstorming sessions where we agreed that Lakmé needed a fresh, youthful image. That's when the idea of Lakmé Fashion Week came about. At the time, fashion weeks were international properties, especially in cities like Milan and Paris, but India didn't have anything like that. We pitched the concept, and Anil Chopra, who was leading the brand then, absolutely loved it. Thus, the Lakmé Fashion Week was born in 1999–2000, and I worked on it for nearly nine years to help establish it as a major event in the Indian fashion world.

We created other successful intellectual properties (IPs) as well, like the IIFA Awards in collaboration with Wizcraft, which has now grown into a global platform for Indian cinema. I also worked with television giants like Sony Entertainment, partnering with industry stalwarts such as Sunil Lulla and Albert Almeida. Today, we work with Zee, but over the years, we've also collaborated with channels like Colors, covering the entire spectrum of entertainment clients.

In the financial sector, we handled major accounts like JM Financial and Kotak. I still remember one of my early meetings with Uday Kotak, when he had just secured a banking licence. He was in the process of envisioning what Kotak Bank would look like and was searching for a solid PR partner to help communicate his vision. We had numerous boardroom discussions about crafting a communications strategy—from how to position the transformation to the launch of the Kotak Bank brand itself, including the design and meaning behind its logo.

I can't even begin to list the numerous issues and crisis work I have handled for clients across industry sectors. While some are well known, others are not—and that's just the way we like it.

In 2007, I decided to become a mother and take a step back—my son would now be my most important 'client'. I informed all my major clients at the time, including Vodafone, Lakmé, BCG, Unilever, Kotak and SET, and they were all incredibly supportive. They all reassured me, 'Deepshikha, take your break, we'll be here when you're ready to return. We're not going anywhere.' So, I took a three-month maternity leave and focused on this new chapter of my life.

As I was nearing the end of my three-month break, I felt the urge to take on something new. I had already led a major city office and built a business, and now was ready for a fresh challenge. Prema, my mentor, asked me what I wanted to do next. I honestly had no clear answer and even considered taking a sabbatical. But Prema wouldn't hear of it. She said, 'Absolutely not. You're not going anywhere.' Instead, she tasked me with helping set up Genesis's public affairs practice.

At that time, public affairs was just starting to take shape in India in a formal way, and we were pioneering the space. My brief was to develop a professional public affairs practice. It took a year during which we had some amazing advisors on board, including Vinay Jha, who was a tremendous mentor. While he knew what clients wanted, we needed to build a team, craft the services we would offer and then figure out how to win business.

Once the public affairs practice was established, I took on the role of chief talent officer. I had always been vocal about the quality of talent in our profession, so Prema essentially challenged me by saying, 'If you're unhappy with it, then fix it.' My problem-solving mindset kicked in, and I eagerly accepted the challenge. It was an insightful move because I had firsthand experience of the skills needed to execute PR campaigns and manage client relations, so it was easy to translate this understanding into building the right learning and development programmes for our teams.

We built the Associate Learning Programme under the Genesis School of Learning to structure employee development. I was responsible for building the organisation structure and the entire employee lifecycle—recruitment, induction, culture alignment, performance management and training. Our company was always known for its strong work culture and ethics, but we had grown significantly by that time. Now we had to institutionalise our culture as we expanded. It's much easier when you're a smaller group, but when you're growing rapidly, you need systems to maintain the values and work style that set you apart.

WPP had acquired our business in 2004 and our focus shifted to preparing for the next phase of growth. My role as chief talent officer was critical in ensuring we had the right people and training in place.

I stayed in the role for about six years until the profession started to change with the influx of global PR firms entering India around 2012–2014. The competition became intense, and we needed to rethink our position in the market. That's when I became the chief marketing and growth officer, another role I created from scratch. Prema encouraged me to design the job description myself, so I did. The focus was on driving new business, developing new services and structuring the organisation for future growth.

Digital was just beginning to emerge as a major trend, so we set up a digital specialisation team and a newsroom for data analytics, which was a groundbreaking service at the time.

Fast forward to 2019 and I was appointed managing director of Genesis BCW after the merger of Burson-Marsteller and Cohn & Wolfe. Prema once again believed I was ready to bring it all together, and I took on the responsibility of leading the combined entity. Some of my colleagues rightly joke that I've done almost every job in the firm except for CFO. These various roles have given me a holistic understanding of the business.

In 2020, I became the CEO of BCW India when we merged Genesis and Six Degrees. More recently, I've stepped into the role of CEO for Burson Group India, following the merger of BCW and Hill & Knowlton. This journey, spanning over thirty years, has been an incredible learning experience, evolving with the firm and the profession as a whole.

The key to leadership is maintaining a growth mindset and working collaboratively. You can't be a strong leader unless you carry people with you. I am fortunate to have an India Management Team, practice chairs and business unit leaders who are today friends beyond colleagues, and we draw strength from our collective experience and expertise. Today, we're a firm of 450 people. While I may not know each one personally, I hope they feel the warmth and connection through the way we engage.

It's about a cascade effect—how I interact with and mentor my immediate twenty-five leaders affect the way they pass that connection to their teams. This helps sustain our culture and sets us apart in the business. Many who leave often return, saying they experienced their greatest learning and growth at Genesis. The work culture they enjoyed here and our quality of client relationships brings them back.

Two things people always mention about us that stand out: learning and culture. At Burson Genesis, we're constantly at the forefront of innovation. Right now, that's AI. We're heavily investing in AI learning programmes. Being part of the larger WPP family has brought tremendous support and learning from other companies in the group, and C.V.L. Srinivas, country manager at WPP, and other leaders are wonderful guides and friends in this journey. The new Burson leaders from around the world and region are bringing in new ideas and fresh perspectives and we are aligned to our purpose of creating value for our clients through reputation.

Continuous learning, a strong ethical foundation and building lasting relationships make us who we are. We consistently prioritise what's right while balancing ethics, governance and respect for everyone.

Knowledge for the Knowledge Economy

Twenty years ago, we launched our flagship learning initiative called the Associate Learning Programme (ALP), the only management trainee programme in India for PR professionals. The success has mirrored the development of the PR profession in India.

The early 2000s marked the rise of India as a leading light of the developing world. The telecom and technology sectors were booming and laying the foundation of a slew of opportunities for growth for many other industries. There was a buoyancy in the country because of the promise of this growth. It signalled to businesses across the world that if they wanted to grow, India was the place to be. The dot-com bubble was building, and though we know in hindsight that there was a course-correction, it forever changed the way we conducted business in general, and marketing in particular. It showed businesses that Indian audiences were ready for the internet and that this could be a great medium to engage with them. A significant shift also came with the rise of online news portals. Suddenly, we had to adapt to a 24/7 news cycle. Information spread faster, and companies needed to be more responsive. We started taking the first steps in digital PR as we began to recognise the power of online platforms to shape public opinion.

For our profession, this meant gearing up with the right expertise and talent to help companies entering India engage with the local stakeholders. In terms of the talent, we realised the need for specialised and customised education. The ALP was set up with that in mind. We equipped various institutions with business insights so that the talent emerging from there would be better prepared to handle the needs of the evolving Indian business landscape.

This was also the period when we became a part of Burson-Marsteller, and by association, a part of WPP. In the mid- and late-2000s, we saw an onslaught of social media. Platforms like Orkut, and later Facebook and Twitter (now X), gave control of information to every person. Each one of us became a potential publisher and every brand a media company.

As communicators, this meant rethinking our approach fundamentally. From paid and earned media, we stepped into the era of shared and owned as well. From controlling messages, we moved to engaging in conversations. Reputation management became more complex, requiring real-time monitoring and rapid response strategies. Realising the need, we set up our centres of expertise for digital and content.

The smartphone revolution in India, particularly in the last decade, accelerated these changes. With millions of Indians gaining internet access through affordable smartphones, the digital divide began to shrink. PR strategies had to evolve to reach this vast, diverse audience. We saw the rise of vernacular content, micro-influencers and hyper-local campaigns.

The lines between PR, marketing and advertising have blurred significantly. In the early 2000s, these were distinct disciplines. Now, we often find ourselves crafting integrated communications strategies that seamlessly blend earned, owned and paid media. Content marketing, once the domain of advertisers, has become a crucial part of PR strategies. In short, PR is now clearly the only discipline that can touch all the stakeholders of a company.

The role of PR professionals has expanded considerably. We're no longer just media liaisons; we've become strategic advisors to C-suite executives. Our purview now includes managing online reputation, crafting thought leadership platforms and even influencing business strategies. This evolution has necessitated a broader skill set, combining traditional PR expertise with digital acumen, data literacy and business understanding.

6

Dhrubajyoti Gayan

Managing Director, Candour Communications

'Our firm is evolving, beyond traditional PR to offer integrated marketing services.'

From Construction Industry to Public Relations

I WAS BORN IN GUWAHATI, ASSAM. MY EARLY YEARS WERE spent moving between cities, since my father was in the administrative service and my mother was a professor. This frequent relocation meant I got to travel and experience different places.

We settled in Guwahati for the later part of my schooling. After that, I moved to Delhi, where I completed my graduation in commerce. I was never very academic, but later completed my MBA.

My professional journey began in the construction industry, where I worked for a few years. Around 1997 or 1998, I transitioned into public relations, joining Perfect Relations, which marked the beginning of my career in PR. This transition was largely influenced by friends in the media business, either in advertising agencies or at television channels, which were just beginning to gain momentum at the time. When I explored career options, I realised that my previous experience wouldn't translate easily into most industries. However, PR was an emerging field, and that presented an opportunity. I have always enjoyed reading and writing, which worked in my favour.

At Perfect Relations, after completing our training, we were asked which area of the business we wanted to join. I told them, 'Anything except technology.' Naturally, the powers above promptly assigned me to the technology practice. In hindsight, I am grateful for that. By the time I left Perfect Relations, I was leading the IT and telecom practice in the Delhi office.

After a couple of years, I moved to Genesis PR, where I initially managed the rapidly growing dot-com practice out of the Delhi office. That of course didn't last long and I transitioned back to the telecom practice.

Thereafter I joined TBWA Anthem, an advertising company, as the head of western region for PR. My wife and I decided to move to Pune from Mumbai, as we were planning to have a child at the time.

After about a year, the then head of PR left the company. Following his departure, I was promoted to the position of India PR Head of TBWA, just before I turned thirty. It was a significant milestone for me—leading a consultancy with seven offices and a team of forty or fifty people within just five years of being in the PR profession.

Over time, I also took on the responsibility of managing the below-the-line (BTL) practice at TBWA, and I remained with the company for about nine years.

Around this time, the people who worked with me—friends and colleagues—kept telling me that they didn't understand why I was still there. In reality, I was already running the firm as an independent business, so why not start something that was really my own? That got me thinking, and I realised they had a point.

In this profession, the barriers to entry aren't particularly high. If you understand the business, have the right people with you and can onboard a few good clients, starting your own firm isn't very daunting. With that realisation, I decided to take the leap. We launched with offices in Delhi, Mumbai, Bangalore and Chennai. We also had people in Kolkata and Coimbatore. Several of our key clients, around eight to ten major businesses, were highly supportive of my new venture.

I reached out to a dear friend who was an Art Director to help me with the name and logo. She told me that, in her opinion, I was the most candid professional she had ever met. That's when she suggested the name *Candour*—and that's how it was born.

The first couple of years were relatively smooth, but as with any business, we faced our share of challenges. We had a pretty rough time for about three years but eventually bounced back. The last ten years have been strong.

The COVID-19 years ended up being a positive phase for us, as the technology sector, especially B2B tech, boomed. Companies that relied on digital solutions thrived, and we were in the right place at the right time. The last five years have been transformative for the B2B tech industry, not just in India but globally. For instance, Zoom became a major business during the pandemic, as remote work and virtual communication became the norm. Alongside that, the need for cybersecurity, data centres and cloud services surged.

Our primary focus has been on the tech B2B segment. One key advantage we had was that, unlike B2C businesses that required physical presence, B2B tech clients were already structured for remote operations. This made it easier to scale without major disruptions.

However, traditional PR, especially media relations, was stagnating, with little to no growth potential. The business was becoming highly commoditised, with many firms competing purely on cost rather than service quality. Recognising these changes, we expanded into social media and digital and marketing services.

Today, we position ourselves as a marketing services-led consultancy. While media relations remain a core part of our business, the larger share of new business in the past couple of years has come from marketing services—lead generation, digital content marketing, design and video production, influencer engagement, and more.

Despite these changes, we've remained a focused, specialised consultancy rather than chasing scale by taking on every kind of work. Our primary clients are multinational tech companies from the US, such as Databricks, OpenText, CyberArk, LDCS and British Telecom, which aligns with our business model. About 70–80 per cent of our revenue comes from global clients, while around 20 per cent is from the Indian market. Naturally we need people who understand technology and we look for people who have either experience in the sector and/or an engineering education.

We have a structured system in place to ensure continuity and efficiency as also to prevent stagnation. Most accounts are led by two senior executives supported by the team made up of people with different skill sets. Having a shadow senior allows for a different perspective and continuous ideation.

Additionally, we maintain a flat organisational structure where communication is open and accessible across all levels. Anyone can speak to anyone.

During the pandemic, we also became completely location-agnostic. Accounts are no longer tied to specific cities—an account in Mumbai isn't necessarily managed from Mumbai, and the same goes for Bangalore or any other location. The focus is on getting the right resources on the job. This flexibility allows us to efficiently handle accounts from various cities, including Pune and Hyderabad, without being restricted by geography.

We've grown steadily through word-of-mouth and client referrals rather than aggressive networking. We also partner with independent PR firms that are globally known for their technology focus. It's a business built on deep relationships and expertise, and at this stage, there's no looking back. The coming years will be challenging for this profession, but I believe we have it in us to use the difficulties to our advantage.

7

Veena Gidwani

Former CEO, Madison Public Relations

'I was blessed to work with talented individuals, each with their unique strengths.'

Five Decades in Marketing Communications and Public Relations

My family's story begins in Karachi, Sindh, before the partition of India. My forefathers were zamindars, owning vast amounts of land, and they lived an affluent lifestyle. All of my father's brothers were highly qualified professionals. After Partition, the entire family relocated to Bangalore, where I was born.

Accustomed to being their own bosses and leading prosperous lives in Pakistan, my family struggled to work for others. They decided to invest in farmland in Bangalore, hoping to continue their independent way of life, but things didn't go as planned, largely because they lacked experience in a new country. Over time, my father and his brothers decided to seek employment. My father, a lawyer, joined the government and worked in the Ministry of Law. His transferable job meant we spent time in Nagpur and with my uncles in Hubli before eventually settling in Bombay when I was about seven years old.

I completed some of my schooling in Nagpur, but most of it was in Mumbai, where I attended Our Lady of Good Counsel School. Initially, I was keen on becoming a doctor, but my parents, concerned about my health and the demanding nature of medical training—especially the internships in rural areas—encouraged me to reconsider. Reluctantly, I gave up on medicine, deciding that if I wasn't pursuing science, I would focus on commerce and management instead.

I did quite well in my SSC exams, which made it easier for me to secure admission to Sydenham College, a top-ranked commerce college at the time. Those four years at Sydenham were some of the most enjoyable and fulfilling years of my life. When they introduced business management as a specialisation, I eagerly chose that path over accountancy or financial management.

I was fortunate to be part of the first batch at Sydenham College to have business management as a specialisation in the third and fourth years. This laid the foundation for my journey in the field of business.

After graduating, I began working as a management trainee with EMT Appliances and Tolbro Cosmetics, a small but reputable company located in Ballard Estate. While working, I also enrolled in a postgraduate diploma programme in Advertising and Public Relations at the Bombay College of Management (KC College, Churchgate). This was a one-year programme designed for working professionals, with classes in the evenings, which allowed me to balance both work and education.

I worked at EMT Appliances for about six to eight months, where I was exposed to various aspects of marketing, from brand development and packaging to advertising. It was an enriching experience as I worked closely with their advertising agency, Heroes Publicity. One day, Heroes Publicity offered me a position, and I decided to join them as an account executive.

I worked at Heroes Publicity for six years and handled accounts for clients like Advani Oerlikon, Bajaj and Westerwork. I gained valuable experience in advertising and client management there. Eventually, Westerwork offered me a position, so I joined them.

However, Westerwork was an engineering company and offered limited opportunities for communication and marketing work. After some time, I decided to move on and joined Firestone Tires, where I was to head their advertising and communication efforts. It was a fascinating experience, as I found myself in a completely different industry—learning how to market tyres. After a couple of years, Firestone was sold to the Modi Group, and the company became Modi Stone. The shift in culture and work environment was significant, and I eventually decided it was time to move on.

I had an offer from the Tata group for Tata Press, which later became Tata Donnelly. Recognising my potential in creative development, Tata set up a creative agency called Design Shop India Limited and asked me to head it. Many of our print clients began entrusting us with creative work, and that went on for some time.

It was during my time at Tata that my journey into PR truly began. I was approached by Pressman Advertising, which was looking to set up a specialised consultancy focused on investor relations, especially with the rise of ADRs (American depositary receipts) and GDRs (global depositary receipts) in the financial markets. I was recommended for the role by Dr Nirmal Suchanti who believed I was the right fit despite my lack of direct experience in investor relations. He reassured me that I would pick it up quickly, and I couldn't resist the opportunity. I had now entered the world of investor relations.

After some time in investor relations, I transitioned into broader public relations with Prima Communications. Following this, in 2000, I joined Sam Balsara to help establish Madison Public Relations from the ground up. We started with just three people, and over the course of twelve years, we grew Madison into a thriving consultancy, expanding to multiple offices with over 100 people. It was a long and rewarding journey, and after a fulfilling career, I decided to step back from full-time work in 2012 and retire, having witnessed and contributed to Madison PR's incredible growth.

My career has spanned an exciting fifty-five years, and I'm still going strong. I started working in 1970, fresh out of college at the age of nineteen. When we started Madison PR, it wasn't easy to acquire clients. Madison Advertising had some business with Procter & Gamble, so we had a small start there. However, everything beyond that was built from scratch. We approached many of Madison's existing clients, like Godrej, but all the pitching, strategies and acquisitions were done independently, which helped us grow organically.

I'd like to highlight a few memorable campaigns that I have worked on. One of them was the launch of Olay Total Effects for Procter & Gamble in 2007. This was a comprehensive campaign centred around the idea that Olay fights the seven signs of skin ageing. Our goal was to educate women that skin ageing begins not at fifty, but around the age of thirty-five. For this campaign, we enlisted six women influencers from diverse backgrounds—Dilshad Pastakia, a hairstylist; actor Tisca Chopra; nutritionist Shikha Sharma; Maria Goretti, and others. These successful women hosted media events where they discussed their personal journeys and the importance of looking good and feeling young. We also had P&G scientists from Bangkok conduct hands-on skin tests for attendees, allowing them to see if their skin appeared younger or older than their actual age. To top it all off, Sushmita Sen was appointed the brand ambassador, and we organised a grand launch event in Delhi that was replicated in other cities.

Another significant campaign was the Shiksha initiative, focused on providing education to underprivileged children. This was one of our first cause-related marketing campaigns, linking marketing efforts directly to corporate social responsibility. For every product sold, one rupee was contributed towards educating these children. All stakeholders participated—dealers, employees, and customers—creating a sense of community around the initiative. Launched with great fanfare, the campaign lasted three months, featuring events every few weeks to maintain interest. Remarkably, Shiksha began in 2005 and continues to thrive even today.

We also collaborated closely with Café Coffee Day to establish its brand identity primarily through PR efforts, avoiding heavy advertising costs. We organised events, coffee plantation visits and book readings in various café formats, creating an active calendar of activities that drove business growth without substantial advertising spending.

In another campaign for Britannia in the mid-2000s, we worked alongside Vinita Bali, who took over as MD during a period of significant reorganisation. After a year of revamping the business, we launched a strategic communication programme to highlight Britannia's new direction, leading to increased recognition and success for both the company and Vinita, who was awarded Businesswoman of the Year by *The Economic Times*. She recognised that much of that success was effectively projected through our communication efforts.

There are so many such campaigns I could mention—if I had the time, I could easily fill a book with them! I've been fortunate to work with really good people throughout my career. I haven't encountered anyone truly difficult. Of course, they had varying levels of capability—some were more skilled, while others had room to grow—but the key for me was to assess people correctly and give them the freedom to prove themselves. I believe in giving people space rather than micromanaging them.

At Madison, I encouraged open communication and collaboration. Our entire team, including trainees, would meet once a fortnight. I included everyone in those meetings, so even the newest hires were aware of every campaign we were working on. We welcomed ideas from anyone, even freshers, and we often received some of our best ideas from them.

One of my core principles was to never let a client down. If we made a commitment, we would move heaven and earth to fulfil it. If for some reason we encountered a problem, we would inform the client well in advance, explain the issue and provide a plan to address it. Surprising clients or leaving them in the dark was unacceptable.

I can recall one specific example. A junior team member and I were to attend a client's annual general meeting in Marine Lines. We left the office with plenty of time, but got stuck in heavy traffic about 1.5 kilometres away. It was 2.35 p.m., and the meeting was to start at 3 p.m. But my colleague had to be there by 2.45 p.m. to set things up. Realising that traffic wasn't moving, he suddenly told me, 'Ma'am, I'm getting off here.' He jumped out of the car and ran across a large maidan, arriving at the venue just in time—perspiring but ready by 2.45. When I arrived at 3 p.m., the client told me, 'Hats off to your team. Your guy made it, and we could see the effort he put in.'

Another value I hold dear is giving credit where it's due. Acknowledging and appreciating people for their hard work and dedication is essential. Madison PR was founded in 2000, and from the very beginning, this spirit of collaboration and commitment was at the core of everything we did.

Throughout my twelve-year journey at Madison PR, I found that we struck a unique balance between professionalism and a family-like atmosphere. Our firm operated more like a family; we celebrated each other's successes and supported one another through challenges. Even during off-site events, we prioritised team bonding and fun, and Mr Balsara often noted how vibrant and close-knit the PR team was compared with other business units.

I was blessed to work with talented individuals, each with their unique strengths. While not everyone had the same capabilities, we leveraged each person's strengths to deliver exceptional results. This collaborative environment fostered long-term relationships with clients like Britannia and Procter & Gamble.

I still work as a consultant, but I also want to explore my personal passions, especially food and playing bridge. I've written a book on food and created over a hundred YouTube videos on the subject. After years of leading businesses, particularly in PR, which is extremely demanding with long hours and constant travel, it was important to carve out time for myself and pursue my hobbies.

PR, a Sophisticated and Strategic Discipline

When I began my career in PR about twenty-five years ago, the field was often misunderstood and underutilised. It was perceived as a superficial exercise involving networking, hospitality and occasionally paying for media coverage. Strategic, planned communication was a rarity, and PR lacked the recognition it holds today as an essential tool for building brands and reputations.

In my early years, PR was predominantly associated with large public sector companies. Their efforts were limited to sending press releases or hosting press conferences, where journalists were incentivised with gifts or cash vouchers. There was little focus on crafting long-term strategies or delivering impactful communication. Press releases were excessively lengthy, uninspiring and more about fulfilling formalities than engaging audiences.

The landscape began to change with the entry of multinational corporations such as Procter & Gamble, Hindustan Unilever and Nestlé. These companies brought a more research-driven approach, integrating consumer insights into their communication strategies. Gradually, PR evolved into a strategic and long-term activity, emphasising clear messaging and meaningful content.

Creativity became central to PR efforts, especially for brand launches. Consultancies began exploring innovative ways to make these events engaging and memorable. For instance, rather than relying solely on celebrities for star power, brands focused on relevance. A food brand might collaborate with a celebrity chef, while a detergent brand could feature an expert on stain removal. The emphasis shifted to delivering research-backed insights and meaningful content, resonating with audiences more effectively.

The concept of influencers also started taking shape during this period. Initially, these were celebrities, but over time it began to include individuals whose credibility aligned with the brand's message. Brands began collaborating with niche personalities—such as social workers or community leaders—who brought authenticity and depth to campaigns, often at a fraction of the cost of celebrity endorsements.

The rise of CSR further transformed PR. Companies preferred not to advertise their philanthropic efforts directly, and PR helped communicate the tangible impact of initiatives like combating malnutrition or supporting children with disabilities. This approach strengthened corporate goodwill and reinforced positive reputations.

Another significant shift came with the emergence of social media in the mid-2000s. Social media revolutionised communication by enabling instantaneous information-sharing, but it also introduced challenges. Negative incidents could quickly spiral out of control, while positive stories could gain massive traction. PR firms had to learn to leverage social media to amplify positive narratives and manage potential crises. This remains a dynamic aspect of PR today.

Cause-related marketing (CRM) emerged as another critical trend. Unlike CSR, which often operates independently of sales, here product sales were tied to meaningful initiatives. Procter & Gamble's Shiksha campaign is an enduring example, where a percentage of sales revenue funds education programmes for children. Such campaigns have grown in scale and impact, demonstrating how PR can align business objectives with societal contributions.

As consumer behaviour evolved, people increasingly sought brands associated with ethical practices and strong corporate reputations. Scandals involving promoters highlighted the importance of nurturing both corporate and brand reputations. PR efforts began addressing these dual objectives, reinforcing trust and credibility.

PR calendars became more comprehensive, encompassing product launches, corporate announcements, annual general meetings and facility inaugurations. These events were strategically leveraged to maximise media coverage and public engagement.

The use of brand ambassadors also played a significant role. Celebrities like Amitabh Bachchan significantly elevated brands through long-term associations, such as his work with Kalyan Jewellers or the Reserve Bank of India's financial awareness campaigns. Sustained, strategically managed partnerships add incredible value to brands, making them essential elements of PR campaigns.

In conclusion, PR has evolved from a reactive, underutilised function into a sophisticated and strategic discipline. The integration of social media, CSR, CRM, influencers and brand ambassadors has transformed PR into a powerful tool for building and safeguarding reputations in a connected world. Today, it continues to adapt to changing landscapes, emphasising meaningful, impactful communication.

8

Santanu Gogoi

Founding Partner, First Partners

'My journey can be an inspiration for every small-town child who has dreams in his eyes and wants to follow his inner calling.'

The Small-town Boy Who Made It Big in PR

I hail from North Lakhimpur, a small town in Assam, the only child of state government employees. I lived there until grade ten, after which I moved to Guwahati to study science in higher secondary school. However, I soon realised that science wasn't really my calling.

For those of us growing up in pre-liberalisation India, there weren't too many professional fields to choose from. Unlike today's India, which is filled with diverse opportunities across vocations, seeking a fulfilling career in a fledgling field required a lot of conviction. With a suitcase full of dreams and the zeal to make a mark for myself, I came to New Delhi for further studies, and the eclectic environment at Delhi University opened up a new world for me. After completing my master's degree in the humanities, I decided to prepare for a career in banking, which I thought would be a good fit for me.

However, I soon discovered that a regular job in the banking sector did not suit my outgoing personality. I craved a profession that allowed for interaction, creativity and movement. At that time, advertising and PR were emerging fields and I got an opportunity to join Clea PR.

My parents, with their conventional career, had reservations at first about this big leap. Peer pressure from family and the community to pursue engineering or medicine was strong. But even in school, I harboured dreams of entrepreneurship, albeit in a vague sense. I used to imagine setting up a conglomerate called 'Gogoi Industries' (a name I fancied as a child).

That dream planted the seed for something big in my future. At that time though, I completed a stint at Clea PR and joined Corporate Voice Weber Shandwick, where I stayed for over a decade and rose to the position of vice-president of corporate practice. For professionals of today's generation, it may seem odd to work at any organisation for over a decade, but it was an enriching experience, offering ample exposure, learning and growth opportunities.

After gaining considerable experience in PR, my entrepreneurial instincts resurfaced. Encouragement from clients and opportunities to start something of my own reignited that old dream. Despite my parents' earlier concerns about the financial capital needed for business, I decided to take the leap.

I knew that the entrepreneurial road would be marked with stretches of uncertainty. My company, First Partners, got off to a rollicking start and was growing every day until the COVID-19 pandemic slowed things down. Like everyone else on this planet, it caught me off-guard, but it was also a great learning experience for me in terms of navigating the uncertainties and managing people and client expectations.

I used the crisis as an opportunity to reimagine things and, accordingly, delved deeper into how First Partners and the PR business at large could adapt to the changing times in a world which is constantly grappling with disruption.

Despite the bumps, I never lost sight of a key goal—fostering a congenial and empathetic working environment at First Partners. I have always been seen as approachable, passionate and concerned about colleagues. The relationships I had developed in the initial stages of my career are still as strong despite time and distance barriers.

Developing close-knit bonds with colleagues and giving counsel to junior colleagues during their trying times are essential for any organisation's sustainability.

I have been part of many award-winning and compelling campaigns involving marquee brands such as ITC, Hyundai Motor India Limited, Rolls-Royce India, McDonald's India and Vedanta. However, one that stands out is the 'Condom Bindaas Bol' campaign for USAID. The campaign won the UN Grand Award in 2007 and was unique in the way it brought together different stakeholders, including celebrities, for a noble, impactful cause. Among the recent campaigns that received global PR appreciation was ITC's Mangaldeep Sixth Sense, which was featured among the top-40 best campaigns at the 2024 Global SABRE Awards.

My journey can be an inspiration for every small-town child who has dreams in his eyes and wants to follow his inner calling.

With technology upending many age-old processes and eliminating human intervention across sectors, my mantra has been to constantly stay updated about developments and always be on the ball. Because a crisis will never knock on the door, it will just be in your face.

Changing Communication Strategies

The public relations landscape, like any other sector, has evolved tremendously over the past few decades with technology coming in as a great enabler as well as a disruptor. In fact, when I look back at the days when I started, I wonder how fast things have changed! I had never imagined that even in a dynamic field like PR, the transition in terms of processes would be so fast.

The way communication strategies are planned now has also changed dramatically since I started out.

PR firms now have to grapple with the strategic shift with regards to paid, earned, shared and owned media. Nowadays, a crisis is just a minute away due to the rapid flow of information across digital mediums and firefighting takes place at multiple levels. So, there is less time to brainstorm solutions.

In the past decade, the print medium was perceived to be the most powerful and effective in disseminating information for achieving business objectives. But now the popularity of digital media outlets and social media influencers has changed consumer habits. This has led to communication and PR plans being tailored accordingly, because one size no longer fits all.

Reimagining content strategy has been the key takeaway for PR firms, and new media like podcast and vlogs have emerged as popular dissemination tools for brands.

Brands also now use localised, relevant content and campaigns to reach out to wider audiences and create buzz. Making the most of this growing trend, influencers now command a significant premium for aligning with brands.

PR thought leadership has also moved beyond simply showcasing products or services. It now seeks to educate, inform and inspire, and is not limited to a particular demographic. Corporate leaders now set the tone through their unique messaging methods on social media. A brand's reputation is now significantly shaped by how its top executive portrays himself or herself. There have been times when corporate leaders have managed to steady the ship by effectively engaging with the media and instilling confidence among stakeholders.

In terms of crafting compelling narratives for brands, data is now becoming a key ingredient. Using analytical tools and charts, data is being strategically used in messaging tools to drive meaningful change.

What I'm sure of, thanks to my two-decade long PR career, is that, no matter the numerous ebbs and flows, the PR profession will navigate deftly through them all. With its core characteristic remaining the same, the profession has stood out for its resilient nature and continues to churn out top-notch professionals who are making the fraternity proud by conceptualising award-winning campaigns and helping clients gain credibility through innovative outreach programmes.

9

Ameer Ismail

President, Lintas Live

'I was fascinated with the world of brands and communications.'

From Hobnobbing with Bollywood Stars to Public Relations

They say that your growing years have a huge impact on your life choices, and that has been true for me too. I grew up in Mumbai living with my grandfather, A.S. Kably, who was a larger-than-life personality. He was always formally dressed, a suit with a crisp white shirt and a bow tie. A big reason for his success as a lawyer was his choice of prominent cases, which always put him in the spotlight. One memory that has stayed with me is finding folders in his office chambers where he had meticulously filed newspaper cuttings. His sharp networking skills helped him get appointed as the consul general of Mauritius. We hosted cocktail parties at home where Bollywood stars and politicians attended to experience my grandfather's charm. All this left an indelible mark on me and subconsciously fuelled my passion for PR (and formal dressing).

As far back as I can remember, I was fascinated with the world of brands and communications. When I was unsure about my career, a relative pointed me to this profession. He said, 'Ameer, you are made for public relations.' He also shared his view that the profession was nascent but had enormous potential. He couldn't have been more right. I am deeply grateful for the early guidance and that gentle nudge into this fascinating world.

After I finished my schooling in Cathedral and John Connon School and college in Jai Hind, I decided to move abroad and study in the US. I even managed to live and work in the UK and Thailand in my early years, and that exposure contributed to my ability to connect with different people and cultures easily.

I joined Good Relations—one of the few PR firms that existed at that time—as an absolute junior. I was ambitious, passionate and always ready to take on any task. This helped me learn the fundamentals and also go beyond them, so I could hone my skills in related areas.

Success came early and I made some strategic career moves in quick succession. With each role came a larger canvas of responsibility. Print media had hailed me as a young, dynamic leader, and getting recognition so early in my career was a heady feeling. I strove always to deliver growth to the organisation I was with.

My final move was to Lintas in 1996 after I met Prem Mehta, who was heading the firm then. My mandate was to build and manage the agency's PR brand, LINOpinion. It was an excellent opportunity, and I accepted the challenge. That was twenty-eight years ago!

My journey has been a dream run, and despite the length of my tenure, I still feel the adrenaline rush when I go to work today. Lintas is one of the best institutions in the business and we provide enormous value to our clients.

In these years, I have been a part of many changes and huge transformations within our group. The PR and advertising business as a whole has also metamorphosed. It is now a very complex ecosystem, and this trend will only continue.

The changes in my role have enriched my career and have allowed me to gain an understanding of different disciplines and various geographies. This includes the exposure to global markets managing PR for MullenLowe across the region as well as leading disciplines like our design business DCell, our event management company Advent, and as the chief growth officer of PointNine Lintas, to name a few. One significant responsibility that I would like to mention here was in structuring a unique partnership with Golin, a sister IPG agency and a global leader in the business. I was invited by Fred Cook (the then CEO of Golin) to be a part of the Global Management Group of Golin during that period.

To create a communications plan or brand strategy, one needs to understand the business, its dynamics and its challenges. I have partnered with some of the best brands and many of these have been long-standing relationships—Starbucks, Porsche, Etihad, Texas Instruments, Visit Victoria, DP World, Rio Tinto and so many more.

I understand the importance of the interventions we suggest and take pride in the tangible results that follow. I love the thrilling ride that is so different every day. This is why I will never hang up my boots or retire.

I have also had the privilege of working with so many respected and amazing colleagues and leaders in Lintas, and must acknowledge their contribution to my journey—Joseph George, Charles Cadell, Balki, Subbu, to name a few from the leadership in creative and PR teams, along with Fred Cook, Ellen Ryan Mardiks, Jonathan Hughes and Matt Neale from Golin and many advertising greats like Mohammed Khan and Ravi Gupta. Rubbing shoulders with these icons helped me understand the diversity of perspectives and the tapestry of talent that makes this profession one of the most interesting ones you can choose.

Prem had told me before I joined, 'Ameer, you will have many careers in one lifetime,' and that became a reality.

The lives of people I have impacted also fill me with pride—one former colleague is currently a professor of communications and PR at a university in the US, another manages celebrities in Hollywood and several others run their own firms.

Staying committed to my work and demonstrating professionalism and humility at every stage are some of the values that have anchored me throughout my journey. As a leader one should up-skill constantly and lead by example. Leaders should do more than state the vision and set goals. They need to show empathy and be willing to roll up their sleeves and be a part of the team in the truest sense. Consultancy life can be stressful and providing a high level of motivation along with the freedom to think and grow without hierarchy, politics or fear is very important. Curating the right culture is critical.

I am incredibly proud of my achievements and am still enjoying every moment of my work. I have reached a point where my purpose is to give back to the firm and the profession.

I believe you should be happy, positive and committed to your own path in life. At this age and stage, my advice to the younger talent is simple: stick to your profession. Even if you need a change, stay in the same stream. Don't look for short-term gains, just connect the dots and stay on your path, and success will follow you.

As the canvas of opportunity in PR continues to grow with digital and AI, deep experiences like mine will still be a necessary ingredient into the PR profession and it cannot be replaced with algorithms.

Scale, Recognition and Relevance

Over the past two decades, PR has achieved scale, recognition and relevance. To share some perspective, globally, there are PR agencies like Edelman and Burson that have over a billion dollars in revenue. This is much larger than many global advertising networks owned by the major holding companies. There are five major holding companies globally: Omnicom, Dentsu, WPP, Publicis and IPG; Lintas is a part of IPG. These giants have multiple PR and advertising brands in markets all over the globe. In India there has been significant scaling of the PR business; many top players have crossed the ₹100-crore revenue mark and while this is relatively small in a global context, there are still enormous growth opportunities in the years to come.

The vast and evolving landscape of digital media has increased opportunities in PR. I attended a meeting in the US where there was a slide shared that stated, 'We scroll through a football field of data daily' and 'we all live in an attention economy and will share only what we care about'. These behaviours became so real for everyone during the pandemic and there is no turning back. Many large media conglomerates are struggling as advertising revenue flows towards technology majors like Meta and Google at the expense of print and television. Therefore, PR practitioners have had to adapt to a hybrid approach to deliver messages while straddling earned media, influencer management and social media. Most agencies have realised that conversations start and get shared online, and that is the space for great insights, forecast trends for clients and start seeding sharable information on relevant platforms. Social listening and online reputation management (ORM) has been embedded into most PR consultancy offerings. This pivot is positive for the profession as consultancies are less focused on relationships with journalists and have moved from intuition to data-driven insights to drive overall strategy. We were one of the first agencies to embed brand planning into our model a few years ago. When you use planning tools backed by research and data, recommendations can be sharp and result in better impact.

A big change I see now is that PR consultancies have realised the importance of creative storytelling, and many global agencies have hired creative leads to fuel the ambition of work worthy of recognition at Cannes. At Lintas Live, we reimagined and recast our model to a creative first digital-led PR consultancy, and that was clearly the right move. The profession is finally getting its right of space at the Cannes Lion Awards. In 2024, Edelman won a Titanium Lion and Golin won a PR Lion Grand Prix for its brilliant Specsavers campaign. Closer home, Indian consultancies are gearing up to win at Cannes with a PRCAI-backed initiative called ‘For the Win’, where some key leaders help consultancy teams upskill to win at Cannes. This trend will continue to blur the lines between what was considered a 'traditional' PR consultancy and a 'creative' consultancy. PR consultancies will go beyond just playing the role of amplification of ideas. What will matter eventually is the effectiveness of the consultancy (creative or PR) in providing solutions and helping solve business problems for clients.

10

Deepak Jolly

FOUNDER, CONSOCIA ADVISORY

'For this profession to grow, we need to create value and have a purpose.'

From Hotel Management to Public Relations

I WAS BORN IN FIROZPUR IN PUNJAB. HOWEVER, MY childhood was spent largely in Delhi. My mother, a teacher and the principal of a high school, and my father, one of the most popular journalists of his time, instilled in me a great value system that is largely responsible for where I am today.

I studied economics along with science in school, and I soon realised that I was far more interested in it than in the science subjects. I also loved to play basketball and chess, and did exceedingly well in both. Though I wasn't much of a singer, I was surrounded by musician friends and joined them in group performances. I grew up to be a great music buff and I've recently rekindled my passion for singing.

I've always had an interest in acting and dramatics as well. As a kid, I was into mimicry and mime but I was unable to pursue it further because of studies and, later, work. However, about eleven years ago, I went back to my love for theatre. Now, I actively pursue it, alongside people like Suresh Narayan, CEO of Nestlé; Aditya Ghosh, co-founder of Akasa; and Rohit Ohri, chairman of the FCB Group. Our theatre group puts on Broadway-style plays. Though we don't have much time for practice, we are allowed to read our scripts during performances. It's a unique form of theatre—spotlighted, short performances lasting around twelve minutes. My wife has also embraced it, making the activity more fun.

After school, I decided to enrol in Hansraj College at Delhi University for an economics honours degree. However, I had also applied for hotel management, and about three months later, I found my name on the waiting list. Why not pursue a professional course alongside my degree in economics, I thought. Moreover, my uncle, Hemant Oberoi, then a renowned chef at the Taj, further influenced my decision, and I began to see hospitality as a viable long-term career. Therefore, I decided to join the Hotel Management Institute.

Our 1981 batch of hotel management was incredibly competitive, filled with some of the brightest students from across India. This competitive environment motivated me to strive for the top. Some of my notable batchmates and friends include Sanjeev Kapoor, the renowned chef, and Puneet Chhatwal, CEO of IHCL.

During my four-year stint in the hotel industry, I quickly realised that if I wanted to carve out a niche for myself, I needed to find the right opportunity. That opportunity came when I transitioned from being a front office manager to handling PR at Le Méridien, Delhi. PR was a natural fit for me. In 1987, Le

Méridien was going through a huge crisis, and that gave me the opportunity to change the perception of the hotel. It turned out to be a success.

During that time, I developed the skill of articulating the company's narrative and my own point of view with clarity and conviction. It's interesting to reflect on how far I had come—from a shy boy to someone confident in speaking and presenting. I had a deep understanding of the hotel industry because of my education and work experience. People noticed the impact I had made, especially because the Le Méridien was a well-known hotel at that time.

Some of the great learnings that have shaped my career:

1. *Listening*: It's crucial to truly listen to your customers.
2. *Honesty*: You must clearly communicate what you can deliver to the client.
3. *Relationships*: Building strong relationships with your superiors, peers and juniors is essential. I was always known as a go-getter because I knew how to get things done by understanding both the task at hand and how to execute it effectively.

After a few years, I realised that I wanted to leave the hospitality sector and continue my journey in PR and government affairs—fields very few people were in at the time. I got selected for a role at Hindustan Unilever, which turned out to be an incredible learning experience. It was the best training ground I could have asked for. At Unilever, I honed several important skills: building consensus, learning best practices, creating processes, aligning diverse teams, and mastering the art of communication. One of my best stints in Unilever was heading the sales team, responsible for a ₹300-crore business.

From Unilever, I moved to PepsiCo India, and from having a task-oriented role, I became a people manager. I learnt the importance of delegation and ensuring tasks were completed efficiently. Over time, I transferred these management skills to public affairs, communications and CSR roles in various large companies like Bharti Airtel, Coca-Cola India and Godfrey Philips.

The biggest satisfaction I have ever derived is from taking social campaigns forward. In 2010, when I was working with Coca-Cola India, we launched a first-of-its-kind campaign in the beverage industry that talked about improving the lives of school children, especially girls. We promoted it on air with NDTV and on the ground with several NGOs across a thousand schools. This campaign was so popular that when we approached Sachin Tendulkar to become our campaign ambassador, he happily agreed.

'Support My School' became one of the best campaigns of my career. Over 100 companies like McDonald's, World Vision, Plan India, Pearson, Luminous Power Technologies and Tetra Pak joined us, and it became a campaign that belonged to everyone, not just Coca-Cola. Support My School made such an impact that Prime Minister Manmohan Singh mentioned it in his speech from the Red Fort, emphasising that every school in India should have toilets for girls. That's the kind of change we were able to bring about between 2010 and 2014. It was truly a proud moment. Such soul-enriching work makes you realise the impact you can make on people's lives.

Throughout my corporate career, the quest to learn never stopped, and I always used to ask myself one question: 'Am I giving my best and can it be done better?' I became an expert in communication, understanding when, how and why to present information. Once you master your job, recognition and success naturally follow. Also, I was fortunate to get the chance to attend the Wharton AMP69 course, a six-week management programme sponsored by my company.

I'm proud that I've reported directly to top management in all my roles. When I conduct training for CEOs, we give them real-world media experiences, simulating TV interviews with tough questions. It's a high-stakes, engaging process. Many CEOs have told me afterwards that nobody had ever asked them such hard-hitting questions. These exercises help them reflect on how they could have responded better, which brings me great satisfaction.

Having reached the peak of my career at fifty-four, I started to think about what I could do next. I was encouraged by friends and colleagues to start a reputation management firm. That is how Consocia Advisory came into being with my two co-founders, Dr Praveen Agarwal and Dr M.V.R.L. Murthy, in 2017. It was born from a genuine desire to make an impact, driven by my passion for communication and people.

My grandmother, who lived to be nearly a hundred, always said, 'The first year will always be the toughest. Don't fall down.' She believed the second year would bring some stability, and by the third year, you'd find success. How right she was! Imagine starting out in a small basement office, handling everything on your own. No business class travel, no luxuries, just hard work and perseverance. But from day one, I made sure we treated our people well, and we became profitable in the very first year. Today, our team has over fifty people, spread across Delhi, Bangalore and Mumbai.

Our first three clients came together serendipitously. One was Tetra Pak, which led us to form the Action Alliance for Recycling Beverage Cartons (AARC), a key association in the recycling sector. Our second client was YourNest, a venture capitalist firm working with start-ups, and we collaborated with five companies from their portfolio. The third client was Select City Mall.

Respect for others is the core of building a good company culture, and it comes from the ability to manage people well. It is a critical skill I've developed. Whether dealing with people, sales or management issues, I've always been called in for my people skills.

I consider my company an extended family, and in my family we respect everyone. I believe that if you give respect, you earn much more in return.

I also focus on building on people's strengths rather than highlighting their weaknesses. I had a team member who was excellent at speaking but struggled with writing and presentations. Rather than criticising him, I helped him improve his presentation skills. Today, he's the CEO of a chess league, and I couldn't be prouder of his success. He regularly sends me messages about his achievements, and it's incredibly rewarding to see him grow. Many early hires, even engineers, have moved on to bigger roles in companies, and they still reach out to thank me. One of the interns I hired went on to become the business development head at Kellogg's, and she sent me a heartfelt message on Teacher's Day, expressing her gratitude.

Throughout my career, I've mentored around twenty-five people, and it brings me great joy to see them succeed. My mentor, the late Suman Sinha, the former CEO of PepsiCo India, had a profound influence on me, shaping me into a better person.

I am known for my passion. If you believe in something and speak about it passionately, people will listen. Be authentic, share anecdotes and don't be afraid to laugh at yourself. These are the values I try to impart to my children as well, and I hope they carry them forward.

Every day, I receive messages from people thanking me for the impact I've had on their thinking and approach. That's what legacy is all about—leaving behind something meaningful for others.

Changing Dynamics of Public Relations

The nature of communication is changing quickly. The trick is to know the right narrative. Way back in 2004, the newspaper industry was thriving and online news had just begun to make its presence felt. The broadcast industry was at its peak and there was no WhatsApp or social media. Things changed dramatically in twenty years. All big newspapers have lower circulation post COVID-19. The number of journalists, from a million in 2004, have come down to less than fifty thousand. Online editions of the newspapers have become far more popular. Social media has also created new content providers who can reach your core audience with more focused messaging, but at the same time can also create nuisance. The viewership of broadcast media has also decreased considerably and the 'WhatsApp factory' is thriving. Gen Z consumes the news online, and on other social media platforms like LinkedIn, X and Instagram. Today's communicators need to be more innovative to gear up to these challenges.

Today, it's all about shaping the narrative—knowing how to tell the right story at the right time makes all the difference. Narratives have become more succinct. You need third-party influencers to tell your story because credibility comes from others speaking on your behalf. For example, a single story about one customer's experience can dramatically impact a company's reputation, as we've seen with stocks taking a hit over a single poor review. That's the power of storytelling and the importance of building trust in others to share your story.

That is why your influencer's narrative is far more important and impactful than your own. Reputation is now also dependent on social media narratives from other people.

The ever-growing influence of social media and other digital platforms has also proliferated a worrisome trend of spreading fake news. In an age where information travels faster than ever, misinformation can spread like wildfire, often outpacing the truth. This is a significant challenge for PR professionals as their profession is built on advocating for the truth. Combating fake news requires a proactive and innovative approach, including swift fact-checks, transparent communication and leveraging credible third-party voices to dispel inaccuracies and settle down rumours. AI is perhaps the best as well as the worst invention of this century as it can dramatically change the narrative both ways.

Every brand is unique in its own way, and the most influential factor that separates them from each other is the narrative. Building a strong narrative is very important, especially today when everyone's in a rush to sell something or the other. Today, the best forms of storytelling have an astonishing ability to create and convey messages that are believable and that add value to millions of people around the world. That's how PR today works. The essence of successful PR lies in building trust and cooperation.

11

Pranav Kumar

Managing Director, India, Allison

'My journey in this field has been extremely fulfilling. I've grown tremendously, both personally and professionally.'

Dreams of Flying Planes and Transformative Campaigns

I was born in Bareilly, Uttar Pradesh, where my father, a fighter pilot in the Indian Air Force, was posted at his home base, as he was on a brief break from active flying duty. My sister and I both spent our early years in Bareilly before we began moving around due to my father's operational flying assignments.

We briefly lived in Secunderabad, followed by a couple of years in Tezpur, Assam. Tezpur, being a crucial Air Force base on the Indo-China border, had a significant influence on my childhood. It was the early 1980s, a time before the internet and cell phones, and living in such a remote area offered a very different kind of life—outdoorsy, adventurous and filled with simple joys. I fondly remember the friendships I made and the exciting times we had.

In 1984 or 1985, we moved to Delhi because my mother wasn't feeling well, and he took compassionate leave. Since then, we've been based in Delhi, as my father decided it was a better environment for my sister and me, especially for our education, with the added support of my mother's family being nearby. My father transitioned to flying commercially, and we settled in Delhi for good.

Growing up around airplanes, I naturally developed a strong desire to become a pilot. My bedroom walls were adorned with airplane pictures and posters, and after finishing school in 1995, my ambition was clear—I wanted to fly. However, my father, with his deep understanding of the profession, advised me against it. The aviation industry was experiencing a downturn, with few opportunities for fresh commercial pilot licence holders. He explained the challenges, including the high cost of education and the uncertain job market, which would make it difficult to sustain a career.

At eighteen, I was unsure of my path, so I decided to attend college at Delhi University, where I earned a bachelor's degree in history. As I was nearing the end of college, I happened to meet a friend's brother, Deepak Agarwal, who was working in PR at the time. Back then, I had never even heard of PR. He was articulate and sharp, and I found myself intrigued by what he did. I asked him about his work and what it involved, and I was captivated by his description. He talked about helping brands and companies engage with the media, acting as a bridge between organisations and the public. Back then, the media landscape was much simpler, and his explanation of how PR operated within that context fascinated me.

At that point, I was still figuring out what I wanted to do with my life. PR came into my life quite unexpectedly, and something about it resonated with me. Maybe it was destiny or just the right timing, but I felt a strong pull toward PR.

Did my parents know about PR? No. Looking back, it's clear that I ended up pursuing a career that had barely begun to take shape in India when I was in school and college. PR wasn't even on the radar as a viable career option in mainstream life then, which makes my journey all the more interesting in hindsight.

I vividly remember those early days. We didn't have a computer at home, and the internet was still a distant concept. So, I carefully drafted my resume by hand. From that point on, my story has been one of persistence, focus and the determination to carve out a path in life. I had a very different plan originally, but by the time I was in my early twenties, my zeal and determination were strong, as they should be at that age.

With no connections in the PR world, I took a straightforward approach—I printed my CV and went directly to the offices of various PR firms. I literally walked in and dropped off my resumé at reception desks. That's how I started looking for a job because I didn't know anyone in the fraternity. I remember visiting firms like Roger Pereira, Lintas (which had LinOpinion) and Good Relations.

I encountered some very kind people along the way. One receptionist at the Lintas office, in particular, stands out in my memory. Her name was Gloria, and she was incredibly friendly. She took my resumé, offered to help and even gave me a phone number to follow up. Eventually, she put my resumé through, and about a year after college, I received a call on our landline while I was taking my dog out for a walk. It was someone from Lintas inviting me to come by for an interview. That's how I landed my first job in PR in 1997.

I was elated about the opportunity to start my career with LinOpinion. In those days, the profession really put you through the wringer. You had to go on media rounds, meet tough journalists, and as a fresh graduate, it was a real test. But that's what life is about—challenging yourself, pushing your limits and trying new things, even when you're nervous and unsure of yourself.

Early on, I realised that I had the ability to get things done. My colleagues and bosses started noticing that I had a certain aptitude, even though I was still so young. Slowly, I began to understand and appreciate the work we were doing. Getting hung up on by rude journalists or dealing with tough clients wasn't great for my confidence, but I kept pushing forward. That persistence paid off, and I managed to find my footing in the PR world.

After my first job, I moved on to Weber Shandwick, which was then known as Corporate Voice. By the early 2000s, I found myself at Genesis, like many others in the profession at that time. Genesis was a fantastic experience, where I got to work with stalwarts like Prema Sagar and Ashwani Singla. For the first time, I saw a highly professional and well-structured organisational set-up, especially at the RK Puram office in Delhi. Ashwani was incredibly smart, and I drew a lot of inspiration from both him and Prema.

I vividly remember meeting Prema for the first time. It was customary for every new recruit to spend a few minutes with her. As a nervous young man, meeting Prema was intimidating. But she immediately put me at ease when she learnt that my father was in the Air Force, like hers. She mentioned that she had a special respect for children from armed forces families because they were raised with simplicity, self-reliance, humility and a strong work ethic. That comment left a lasting impression on me.

At that time, PR was still in its infancy in India. Genesis, at least from my point of view, played a crucial role in convincing Indian companies—since there weren't many global companies operating here yet—of the importance of investing in PR and reputation management. But after spending three or four years in the profession, I began to feel restless. I started questioning whether I wanted to continue in PR, especially since my work involved a lot of routine tasks like faxing press releases, making calls and going on media rounds. I wondered if there was more to life and decided to explore other opportunities.

In my mid-twenties, I took a bold step and moved away from PR firm life to experiment with something different. I joined IMG, the sports marketing firm now known as IMG Reliance. Sports marketing was a relatively new concept in India, and as a lifelong golf enthusiast, this field appealed to me. IMG was the largest and most influential sports marketing company globally, representing legends like Andre Agassi, Michael Schumacher, Arnold Palmer and, of course, Tiger Woods. Mark McCormack, the founder of IMG, was an inspirational figure who had written books like *What They Don't Teach You at Harvard Business School*. I was incredibly impressed by the company and excited to join them.

During my three-year stint at IMG, I was involved in various aspects of sports marketing, from managing events to working on client representation and sponsorships. We handled high-profile clients like Leander Paes and Ajay Jadeja, and had a major television arm called TWI, which was the world's largest producer of sports programming content at the time. My background in PR gave me a unique perspective on how brands leveraged sports sponsorships, events and activations. Because of this, I often found myself working on the PR aspects of these sponsorships, advising brands on how to maximise their exposure.

While working at IMG was an exciting and glamorous experience, I eventually realised that sports management was still a niche field in India. Apart from IMG, most other companies in the space were small, promoter-run set-ups with limited growth potential. I felt like I had hit a wall after three years. Still in an experimental phase, I decided to make another significant change. I left IMG and joined Sapient, a technology and IT outsourcing company that is now known as Publicis Sapient.

At Sapient, I worked in an internal marketing role, primarily focusing on business development intranet for the company. This project required a lot of writing and content creation, playing into my natural strengths. Even though Sapient wasn't conducting business in India at the time, I often supported various initiatives, from internal communications to some external marketing efforts.

I was part of the broader employee advocacy group, and I got to try many different things. I loved the global experience Sapient offered. It was my first time working in a truly international set-up, and collaborating with colleagues and stakeholders from Europe and the US. This exposure taught me how large technology services companies like Sapient operate, while working with clients like United and American Airlines. I learned a lot about customers' journeys and marketing strategies in a global context.

However, despite this valuable experience, Sapient's India operations at that time weren't as externally focused in India, which contrasted with the more in-market roles I was in previously. So I found myself at a crossroads, when I was around thirty, contemplating my next move. It was simple: I should return to what I was good at—communications and PR.

By then, the internet had taken off, and PR had also evolved significantly since I first started in the late 1990s (no more faxing press releases!). Maybe PR had become 'cooler' than before. I reached out to Ashwani Singla over email and he asked me to rejoin Genesis. That's how I got back into the mainstream consultancy world.

I had the opportunity to work with some fantastic brands during that time—Motorola, Boeing, Iffco-Tokyo, Avaya, Singapore Airlines—and even played a role in the early stages of Indigo's formation, where I worked with their American CEO. It was a pivotal period, and it reaffirmed my decision to return to PR and communications.

I vividly recall visiting the Indigo office and spotting aircraft seats in the lobby. At that time, they had just finalised their flight number, 6E. The CEO was excitedly announcing, 'We have 6E!' All the journalists present there shared a laugh—'Oh yeah, 6E, cool!'

That experience truly revitalised me. I found the work environment exciting, especially getting to collaborate with CEOs and leaders. But I wanted to take on more responsibilities, which is why I decided to pursue a role at a more niche consultancy firm where I believed I could make a more meaningful impact. I joined Gutenberg, which was a relatively new firm back in 2006–2007.

My true journey began at Gutenberg—not only in servicing clients but also in pushing my own limits and, for the first time, involved in growing a business. I needed to stay focused on my chosen path, and I poured my energy into the role. Within my first year, I was effectively running the firm's India operations, significantly growing the team and its India business. It was my first time managing the business side of a PR firm, and I found it to be incredibly enriching.

Encouraged by this success, I moved on to establish the India business for Bite Communications, which is part of the Next 15 Group that includes Archetype (the erstwhile Text100). I became its first employee in India in 2011 and set about building the team from scratch. While it was intimidating at first, I remember feeling confident by my bold move. By then, I had found my sweet spot in balancing client consulting and running a business.

I genuinely enjoy consulting—working directly with clients and being a valued advisor—while also relishing the complexities of managing a P&L and driving business growth. It's definitely not for the faint-hearted. In consultancy life, rejection is part of the job, and running a business presents even more challenges—from budget cuts to client attrition and talent acquisition.

The team and I successfully grew Bite until the Next 15 Group decided to merge it with Text100, at which point I continued to manage the business within the larger organisation. Eventually, I was presented with the opportunity to start Allison from the ground up in India. In 2017, I became employee number one again, advocating for our entry into the market.

I still vividly remember my first day at Allison—I set up my new Dell laptop at home and took a picture, captioning it 'New beginning'. It was a fresh start, and I was excited for the journey ahead.

Since then, I've grown this business faster than any of my previous endeavours. This growth has been fuelled by my experience and the immense opportunities present in India, where communication and PR have evolved into a highly valued and recognised function that is essential for management in any organisation.

The past seven to eight years have been incredibly enriching—expanding the team, acquiring new clients and building a business from the ground up. Would I want to do it all over again? Probably not, as it requires immense energy and focus. But I thrive on challenges. I love them! I recall a moment in my second or third year of Allison when I was in a conference room on a call. I looked back to see the team engaged in a lively conversation and laughing together. I realised how far we'd come—from just me with a laptop to a vibrant team. Every new hire brought special excitement because we were building something meaningful and growing together.

My journey in this field has been extremely fulfilling. I've grown tremendously, both personally and professionally. Each step required me to push my boundaries—whether it was speaking on panels, representing the company or working with diverse clients who expect complex counsel and solutions. I have been privileged to work on some of the world's best brands and with amazing people from around the world.

Currently, 99 per cent of our portfolio at Allison consists of global brands operating in India, and they rely on us for solid advice and guidance.

Looking back on my long years in consultancy leadership, I couldn't have asked for anything more. I'm incredibly grateful for the opportunities I've had. This is my chosen path, and I intend to continue with it.

Currently in India, we are truly riding the wave created by pioneers. In recent years, PR has come of age, and we're all benefiting from this evolution. Today, it is in a much different place than when I first started. There are more consultancies, a certain commoditisation of the profession and challenges related to global headwinds and geopolitical issues that affect client spending on external communications services. While India remains a growing market, navigating this landscape requires all the experience I've gained over the years.

One of the campaigns I'm most proud of is the launch of TikTok in India. We started our work with TikTok when it was still a little-known app called Musical.ly. ByteDance, TikTok's parent company, hired us to conduct some outreach for Musical.ly. Then one day, we received the exciting news: 'Hey, Pranav and team, we're merging with an app called TikTok. Tomorrow morning, we'll officially be TikTok, and here's the press release.'

We began working with them around 2018, and our team played a crucial role in making TikTok and short-form video a phenomenon. The platform's rise coincided with the surge in popularity of short videos, which posed a challenge to established social media companies like Facebook (now Meta). I can confidently say that we were instrumental in bringing short-form video content into the mainstream conversation and elevating the platform's profile.

Throughout our collaboration, we executed numerous campaigns for TikTok. One of the most memorable was centred on the idea that while TikTok was primarily known for entertainment and fun 'LOL' videos, it also had a significant educational aspect. We noticed a growing trend of influencers using TikTok to share valuable knowledge, from financial advice to educational content.

Recognising this opportunity, we launched a campaign using the hashtag #EduTalk, which highlighted TikTok as also a platform for learning. We showcased how users could engage with academic subjects and improve various aspects of their lives—be it financial literacy or health tips—through TikTok.

We identified top influencers and trending themes within the #EduTalk initiative, and it turned out to be an award-winning campaign. It was groundbreaking because it shifted the perception of the brand.

Leadership is a journey of self-discovery and continuous learning. While we all have a particular style, it's essential for a leader to keep evolving and looking for ways to serve their team better. My approach to leadership has always been about empowerment.

I've never prioritised seniority over talent and ability. When I recognised someone's potential, regardless of their age or experience, I trusted in their skills and competence, and encouraged them to take the lead with clients, even if they weren't considered 'senior'. I've always challenged the corporate world's bias that you're either too young or too old. To me, it's about ability, because age is just a number.

For instance, I would often tell my younger colleagues, 'No one told Mark Zuckerberg he couldn't start Facebook just because he was seventeen.' He believed in his idea and moved forward because of his talent and creativity. I've always seen my role as a leader to identify such potential, guide and mentor it, but also step back and trust people to grow and lead.

At the core of my leadership style is fostering trust, giving people space and enabling their growth.

Equanimity is one of my core tenets. As a leader, your team looks to you for reassurance. You can't afford to panic or lose composure in tough situations. Your demeanour sets the tone for the entire team. Equanimity, therefore, is one of the most vital qualities of effective leadership.

A few years ago, I had the chance to attend executive education programmes at the Wharton School, University of Pennsylvania, USA. I arrived on campus and stumbled upon a quote by Joseph Wharton, the famous American industrialist and founder of the eponymous B-school. He said, 'Forge into the future with courage and without hesitation and delay to go collect your reward.' Those lines stayed with me and have since guided me all this way.

We've Come a Long Way from Faxing Press Releases to Emailing Them

The past two decades serve as an ideal horizon to reflect on where the Indian PR profession is today. At first, we saw the adoption and growth of the internet. Remember that the early 2000s were relatively nascent years where businesses and the workplace rapidly transformed. As a sidenote, we went from faxing press releases to emailing them! Then there was the 2008 global slowdown, which tested many firms. It was akin to the economic volatility we frequently face today. Challenging, cyclical moments make industries resilient and, like most others, the PR business emerged more adaptive.

Simultaneously, the emergence of social media and digital platforms at that time was similar to the arrival of artificial intelligence today, a critical inflection for the PR business. And lastly, the inescapable COVID-19 pandemic, a crisis like no other, once again redefined the profession with communications emerging as a vital business function. Clearly, a lot to pack in!

India's relatively young PR profession evolved against this backdrop, emblematic of the increasing volatility we are subject to and providing valuable lessons as we look into the future. Since all of these areas have been expounded enough, I thought it's best to offer a ringside view of how I saw the profession change over a two-decade consultancy career.

There is acceptance and recognition of PR as an essential part of the marketing mix. That was not always the case in the early to mid-2000s, a time where PR was seen as advertising's poorer cousin. We were literally relegated to being the last few slides on a brand strategy deck or of an integrated ad-agency pitch. As was often said, 'Here's the research, brief and strategy, just add the PR slides.' I can only imagine the perception challenge that consultancy founders and leaders had to surmount. Fast forward to 2024, that is no longer the case (for the most part). India's expansive media industry, and the proliferation of digital channels and an increasing propensity for issues and crises, makes PR a no-brainer for the most mature organisations as well as savvy, new-age brands.

These two decades also saw India's PR firms (both local and global) adapting a fast-changing mainstream and social media landscape where journalists were not the only voices or 'influencers' anymore. As communications became more unidirectional, they put the power in the hands of the consumers. This precipitated an identity change from PR to communications. Full-service firms began to be seen as strategic advisors with integrated communications offerings to handle the onset of user-generated content, or social media. Fast-paced digital adoption meant a changing buyer journey and the word 'influence' assuming a newer meaning. The growth of online communities and new-age platforms such as blogs and online news media meant that we as practitioners had to develop more segmented outreach strategies with bespoke messaging. These were foundational changes, a precursor to what our world looks like from a communications point of view.

Lastly, nothing solidified the role of communications more than the pandemic. That's when organisations fully understood and appreciated the very foundations of PR and when communications teams, whether in-house or consultancies, took the lead and built impactful engagement, fostering trust and transparency while balancing business priorities and altruism.

If the past two decades are anything to go by, one can only imagine what the next two will look like. I am inspired by how far we have come and there is no doubt that technology will disrupt an anyway fast-changing world. The only thing I know for sure is that we as a profession will always rise up to that challenge.

12

Sonya Madeira

Founder, Rice Communications

'"I am going to be a public relations consultant when I grow up," said no one ever.'

A Half-Mumbai, Half-Delhi Girl Who Built Her Career in Singapore

I was born in Mumbai in 1973. I grew up between my grandmother's house on Nepean Sea Road, and Delhi, where my parents were based, with two years in Agra thrown in. An only child, I spent a lot of time reading or going to the club for a swim after school. It was an unconventional upbringing for sure. My entire family was involved in the music industry in some way or the other. So, there was always music and musicians in the house.

The longest I spent at school was at the Convent of Jesus and Mary in New Delhi, where I made some life-long friends. From there, I headed off to Lady Shri Ram College to pursue a bachelor's degree in English literature. We had moved from

Defence Colony to Gurgaon, and what stands out in my memory the most is the long commute to and from college.

After graduation, I was keen to study further. I wasn't clear about what career options I could pursue and joined the Times School of Marketing for a year-long post-graduate programme. Public relations had been one of the modules we covered. It was a good course, affordable by many standards and just a year long. Once again, I made so many dear friends here. An indelible memory is going to the *Times* printing press, watching the newspaper being printed, loading the trucks at 4.00 a.m. and following the delivery routes.

It was a chance conversation with a classmate that got me thinking about a career in PR. They had started working at a PR consultancy straight after university and suggested that I come in for an interview. That was my first meeting with Prema Sagar and her team at Genesis PR. I walked into their office in Aradhana Enclave to understand what a career in PR entailed. The other option was to sell space in a business magazine, which didn't sound very appealing.

I am glad I opted for the PR route. I began working in 1995 with a starting salary of ₹3,500 per month. It was my first real job, and I was both nervous and excited. The PR profession was fairly new at the time. Prema Sagar had recently set up Genesis PR, and the big clients in those days were The Park Hotels, DCM Daewoo, Discovery Channel, RPG Ricoh, Perkin Elmer and so many more. (Last year I had coffee in London with a professional connection who said he was the client at Perkin Elmer in India in 1996—what a small world!).

There was so much learning, and I was so eager to please. Prema was an amazing leader, and she pushed all of us in different ways to learn quickly and be the best. She remains the undisputed Grande Dame of the business, and provided a training ground and strong foundation for so many leaders in the profession: Deepshikha Dharmaraj now leads Burson India, Archana Jain helms Havas PR Pundit, Nandita Lakshmanan runs The PRactice, Nitin Mantri leads Avian WE. These are just some of the people I worked with.

From there, I moved to Text100 India, which really was an incredible place to be at the time. We welcomed Bill Gates to India (multiple times), launched Microsoft Office and Internet Explorer and serviced SAP. Some of my strongest friendships date back to this time when we worked hard and had each other's backs.

At this time, I had followed my ex-boss to a content company he founded. The timing was off and a couple of years later, the company went under during the dot-com bust of 2001–2002. At that time, there weren't any interesting opportunities in consultancy leadership in India. My parents had already migrated to Australia, so I took a chance and applied to a couple of PR firms in Singapore.

Singapore was a different kettle of fish—it was quite a shock to move, which I did with one suitcase. I got to work at Hill and Knowlton and Weber Shandwick before realising I enjoyed the entrepreneurial mindset of a smaller firm. I got to put my learning to work at a local firm for a few years, and in 2009, gathered the courage to set up Rice Communications.

I call myself an accidental entrepreneur. I didn't have this great vision of starting my own business. In fact, I really was so comfortable working for others. But when the stars align, you follow your destiny.

I remember day one at Rice at a client event in Sentosa, with a laptop, a mobile phone and two colleagues. It was such a liberating feeling, yet nerve-wracking at the same time. When you start from the bottom, the only way is up! In February

2025, we were more than seventy talented employees across six offices in the region, incredible clients and a full suite of services.

I would definitely count a solution-oriented mindset as having played a big role in my career, always asking the client what their problem was and coming up with ideas to resolve it. This way, we were able to gain so much non-linear experience and learnt even more from experts in other fields.

I also think empathy is quite high, so I was always happy to help start-ups, partners, non-profits, and even employees looking to move on—hopefully karma comes back in some form or other. Each year we would support a pro-bono or discounted client. This really laid a strong base for us, and made us a consultancy with heart.

I think I was also open to giving people a chance, since I appreciate those who took a chance with me. This resulted in both long-lasting colleague relationships as well as those with clients and partners.

I tried my best to trust people to get the job done. This worked in most cases, but sometimes it backfired. And I had to slap my non-confrontational self into action. Where it did work, people were able to forge their own paths.

Overall, a people first, profits later approach is how I set up the business. Having said that, we were profitable from the first year, and continued growing every year.

I would say the work around the first Bill Gates visit to India is indelibly inscribed in my memory. The ATL and BTL agencies were briefed together, and no one was pedantic about who came up with the idea. We were involved in everything, from internal townhalls, meetings with government officials, partners, clients, media and analysts. Sadly, very few clients work like this in current times.

More recently, the Voices for Momos campaign by RICE Myanmar for World Wildlife Fund was a favourite. It was created in response to the growing elephant poaching crisis in Myanmar. Today, illegal wildlife trading markets have been shut down, and more organisations have committed to continuing the efforts.

On 28 February 2025, we closed a deal to sell the business to Finn Partners, which also happened to be my last day at the firm.

13

Sunayna Malik

Managing Director, Archetype, India

'Balancing being a tough taskmaster with sensitivity, I aim to create an environment where challenges become opportunities and people can thrive.'

From Marketing Communications to PR Consulting

I was born in Delhi, where my father, a senior economist and joint secretary in the Ministry of Agriculture, inspired my interest in how events like the monsoon and wars impact the economy. My mother, an early B.Ed. graduate, focused on our education at home and instilled discipline in me as the eldest of three siblings. My love for reading was nurtured by my maternal grandfather, who gifted me *Reader's Digest* subscriptions. I attended the Convent of Jesus and Mary, a prestigious school in Delhi.

When choosing a career, I was torn between medicine and literature. While preparing for medical entrance exams, an unsuccessful attempt led me to switch to literature at Kamala

Nehru College. Persistent, I convinced the principal, Dr Gorawara, to grant me admission despite closed applications, and with my mother's reluctant approval, I made the change. I loved studying literature and pursued a master's degree at Hindu College, but the idea of journalism, first suggested by my grandfather, lingered. I applied to IIMC, where a spirited interview debate surprisingly earned me admission. After graduation, I interned with Doordarshan to explore field reporting, declining a desk job from *The Times of India* despite winning an award.

My first role as a correspondent at *Centre Magazine* in Delhi marked my entry into the dynamic world of journalism. I began with city-centric content before transitioning to business writing, covering prominent Delhi business houses and building corporate connections. Later, I managed a small advertising and design unit, overseeing creative projects, pitching for new business and leading a team. This role introduced me to the essentials of business growth, like recruitment, discipline and team-building.

While my family urged me to consider marriage, I prioritised career growth, aiming for a managerial position to secure my ability to continue working post-marriage. My father supported this plan, and I eventually joined Modi Xerox as the marketing communications manager.

My boss soon quit, leaving me to navigate the joint venture between Rank Xerox and the Modi Group independently. It was a challenging yet rewarding experience, exposing me to corporate dynamics, senior executives and expats. I managed communications, collaborated with ad agencies and handled everything from messaging and brochures to brand positioning. This role honed my skills in advertising, marketing and corporate communications.

I stayed at Modi Xerox for six to seven years, during which I got married and moved to Mumbai as my husband was based there, heading the West Zone for Eternit Everest. Xerox transferred me to Mumbai as their training and marketing lead and I worked closely with the sales team, gaining hands-on market experience. I was involved in launching the fax machine, leading training sessions and teaching the Xerox sales method—a fulfilling role.

After my first son was born prematurely, I took a break to care for him. During this time, I received an unexpected call from Ashok Jain at EKIM, which was part of the RPG Group. Despite being on maternity leave, Ashok's flexibility allowed me to work from home initially, a rare practice then. In a few months, I joined EKIM as corporate and marketing communications lead, balancing work and motherhood.

As my son's health improved, I transitioned to full-time work and stayed with the company for nearly four years. During that time, the RPG Group expanded into mobility, landlines and paging services. When my husband was transferred to Delhi, I initially stayed in Mumbai for six months before relocating.

In Delhi, I continued working with the Mumbai team, travelling weekly. I'd take an early flight, work with my boss and return by evening. Despite the hectic schedule, my supportive bosses made it manageable, offering remote work options ahead of the times.

During this period, I had my second son and transitioned to HCL, encouraged once again by Ashok Jain, who had moved there. At HCL, I initially reported to Ashok before working with Vineet Nayar Jr., head of HCL ComNet, during the lead-up to HCL Technologies' IPO. My role in IPO communications introduced me to investor relations and brought me into contact with Shiv Nadar, an experience that was both intimidating and enlightening. In my first meeting with Nadar, I struggled to follow the discussion, but his sharp mind and high expectations quickly became evident. Working with leaders like Nadar and Nayar taught me about discipline, strategic thinking and adaptability.

During this period, I handled key tasks like writing HCL's annual reports, which required precision and creativity to meet exacting standards. By the time I completed my third report, I began questioning my career trajectory. Despite heading communications, I felt I was repeating similar work and started considering a move into consulting for a fresh challenge.

Just as I was thinking about it, opportunities seemed to align naturally. I shared my profile with headhunters, and one led to an interview with Text100, a company I knew well from my IPO days. I had a good rapport with Zach James, and during our candid meeting at the Oberoi, he joked about the redundancy of using a headhunter since we were already in touch. Text100 was considering me for a senior consultant role to lead their largest account, Microsoft. After discussions with Zach and Rishi Seth, I had to interview with Microsoft's marketing head, Ranjit Singh. Despite limited preparation time, the interview went well, and Ranjit approved my appointment, marking my move to the consultancy side.

I had worked extensively with various consultancies at HCL during the IPO phase. This exposure gave me a strong understanding of PR strategies and how firms like IPAN, 20:20 MSL, Weber Shandwick and Genesis operated. By the time I formally entered the PR field, I had a well-rounded perspective on the profession.

At Text100, my first months were eye-opening, as consulting from the firm was very different from the client's perspective. Managing a large team for Microsoft, with about twelve seasoned professionals, was challenging. Many had years of experience on the account and deeper day-to-day client knowledge. I had to quickly adapt, learn and prove my value in a demanding environment.

The team, mainly composed of exceptional women, was passionate and protective of their work. It was a trial by fire for me, especially when I was tasked with preparing a crucial briefing document in the absence of the senior lead. Completing it by midnight taught me about the complexity and expertise the role demanded.

This experience improved my rapport with the team, and we delivered innovative work together. One major highlight was managing Bill Gates' visit to India, which included meetings with the prime minister, CEO sessions and high-profile engagements. For the first time, I involved the entire team in different aspects of the visit, ensuring everyone gained valuable experience, despite some resistance from the corporate account directors who traditionally handled such events.

Over the next few years, we continued to excel for Microsoft. On a personal level, I moved from a private office at HCL to an open, vibrant workspace at Text100, surrounded by a young, dynamic team. The culture and camaraderie made the adjustment worthwhile. When Rishi and Zach moved on, there were concerns about Text100's stability, but as head of the Delhi office, I helped navigate the transition. I initially declined the role of managing director to focus on my son's twelfth-grade board exams but accepted it two years later once he was in college. Leaders like Eva Lawlor helped me see that my role was to enable my team, not do everything myself.

In the last seven to eight years, I've embraced this leadership approach, focusing on growth, troubleshooting and providing strategic counsel for complex accounts, particularly in the tech sector. My tech background has been invaluable in understanding clients like Cisco, Microsoft, Ericsson and IBM. My priority has been growing the company while preserving its culture of camaraderie, care and fun. Balancing being a tough taskmaster with sensitivity, I aim to create an environment where challenges become opportunities and people can thrive. Text100 taught me the value of a supportive, dynamic workplace, a legacy I strive to uphold.

My priorities have always been clear: growing the business, keeping the team together and mentoring high-potential individuals. I believe in serving clients with integrity, ensuring our work aligns with the broader ecosystem. I've made tough decisions, walking away from clients who were disrespectful or unwilling to fairly compensate us, even if it meant ending long-standing relationships. I've always stood by our worth. Work–life balance is also important, and while we're available during crises, we value planning time and respecting weekends. I respect my team's leadership and their growth into dependable professionals. With a strong company culture and global support, we have the autonomy to make decisions, which is both empowering and pressuring. We remain ambitious, constantly seeking new opportunities, adapting as PR evolves. The journey is far from over, and I'm excited for what's ahead.

14

Nitin Mantri

Regional Executive Managing Director (APAC), WE Communications, and Group CEO, Avian WE

'I've evolved as a leader over time. Running a firm with five employees is very different from working with a team of five hundred.'

First Ever ICCO President of Indian Origin

I was born and raised in Delhi, where my father worked as a political journalist and my mother a Hindi teacher at the School for the Blind for Girls, eventually retiring as a principal. I am the youngest of three siblings. My elder sister, a doctor, is now based in the US, while my other sister teaches at a school in Delhi.

Growing up in a home with a journalist father meant I was constantly surrounded by newspapers and discussions on media, politics, policymaking and the role of journalism in society. My father had a strong socialist influence, which shaped many of our conversations at home. On the other hand, my mother's academic background instilled a sense of discipline and intellectual rigour. The combination of my parents' professions created a unique environment that fuelled my curiosity about both the media and education.

I completed my schooling at Springdales School on Pusa Road. For college, I attended Venkateswara College at Delhi University in Dhaula Kuan. Later, I pursued an MBA from the Birla Institute of Management and Technology (BIMTECH).

If I hadn't pursued a career in public relations, I would have become a banker or a chartered accountant (CA). In fact, I almost joined Andersen, which was a major global auditing firm before it split into Andersen and Accenture. I had the opportunity to do my articleship with them while completing my graduation and preparing for the CA exams. I even spent a day there but decided not to continue. I thought I'd consider this option after graduation instead of pursuing it alongside my studies. So, in a different world, I probably would have become a CA or a banker. But life took a different direction.

After graduating from BIMTECH, I got a job at a leading computer company. However, many friends and colleagues encouraged me to explore PR, pointing out that I had the right communication and writing skills for the field. At that time, I was active in my local community in Gulmohar Park, doing everything from running a small book club and organising social events to managing a lending library from home and helping publish a local magazine called *Expressions*. These experiences sparked my interest in PR, and I believe that's also when my entrepreneurial spirit first began to take shape.

Eventually, I decided to give PR a shot. I interviewed at both Genesis and IPAN and met both Prema Sagar and Rajiv Desai. Although both jobs offered a lower salary than my current position at the computer firm, I felt it was the right path for me and decided to make the switch.

Early in my career, I sought advice from a highly respected figure in the communications field, Dilip Rangnekar, who was then the head of corporate communications at a major company. He advised me to join Genesis PR, suggesting that a smaller firm would offer more opportunities for hands-on experience and learning. Thus began my journey at Genesis PR when they were still based in RK Puram. With an MBA in both marketing and finance, I brought a well-rounded understanding of both disciplines to the company, which allowed me to make more informed, strategic decisions.

PR stalwarts Archana Jain, Nandita Lakshmanan, Geeta Singh and Deepshikha Dharmaraj were already with the company when I joined. Nandita soon moved to Bangalore, while Archana, Geeta and Deepshikha were still in Delhi, though Deepshikha was preparing to relocate to Mumbai. During my interview process, Archana told me, 'You know we only have women here, right?' Later, Geeta asked me the same question. I remember thinking, 'Why do they keep asking this? Should I be worried?' But I assured them it wasn't an issue.

I often talk about how I was the first male employee at Genesis. In the conference room at lunchtime, I'd find myself sitting with fifteen or twenty women who were all watching *Santa Barbara* on TV. I wanted to watch cricket, but since I was the only one interested, I didn't stand a chance! At the time, I was twenty-three, unmarried and feeling a bit out of place. It was only when another male colleague, Ganesh, joined that we finally adjusted our lunch timings to accommodate our mutual interest in sports.

My first press conference was a memorable experience. The event was held at the Oberoi in Delhi for a client called

Nippon. My boss at the time, Sheena Sharma, gave me clear instructions: 'Take a car, go to the INS building, pick up all the media persons and bring them to the press conference.' I followed her instructions to the T.

Though I initially joined the Delhi office and worked there for a year, I spent most of my time at Genesis in Mumbai. They needed someone from Delhi to take over when Deepshikha, who had relocated to Mumbai, was preparing to move abroad.

I was excited when I was asked if I'd like to permanently move to Mumbai. I agreed if they would cover my living expenses. Genesis was extremely supportive, and I made the move. In Mumbai, I was one of two people co-running the office. I lived in Bandra and worked in Worli—it was great fun, and I really loved the city. I still do!

I spent four years in Mumbai before landing the Microland job, which led me to shift to Bangalore. It was time to give a new city and a new opportunity a shot. That it was in the tech space was a bonus. I spent about ten months there. However, later that year, I made the decision to move to London, where I spent the next six to seven years. This wasn't in my plans, but my wife had gone to the UK in 1999 to pursue her MBA at Leeds University. After finishing her one-year course, she wanted to stay back and work in London. She suggested I apply for jobs there, and eventually, we both secured positions in London. So, being there was a result of circumstances.

In the UK, I worked with Omnicom, initially at a consultancy called Brodeur, which later became Pleon and eventually Ketchum. I left the firm before it transitioned to Ketchum. My time at Brodeur/Pleon lasted from 2000 to 2006.

I got the job at Brodeur with Prema's help because it was a former partner consultancy of Genesis. I asked her for an introduction, and she kindly agreed, leveraging her connections to help me. The firm was tech-focused, and since back then, not many people in the UK had a deep understanding of the tech industry, I was in the right place at the right time.

After six years in the UK, I started feeling the pull to return to India, driven by a desire to become an entrepreneur. A mutual friend, Sharif Rangnekar, introduced me to Nikhil Khanna. Nikhil had already established Avian in India, and Sharif suggested we partner together to build something bigger.

Interestingly, Prema had also recommended I speak with Nikhil, as she believed there was potential in collaborating with him. Nikhil and I met in London, had some great conversations and eventually I visited India to meet him again. While Sharif didn't join the venture, Nikhil and I decided to move forward.

I returned to India in 2006 and became an equal partner with Nikhil in Avian, which had already been operating for about a couple of years. The transition from London, where everything was highly organised, to India's more 'thriving in chaos' style was a significant adjustment. In India, the challenge was to find ways to create processes amid the chaos and working around them while implementing structure where possible. I also learnt valuable lessons in marketing myself and managing work efficiently—lessons I have carried with me throughout my career.

Before joining Avian, I had built a solid foundation in my previous roles. At Genesis, I gained extensive experience managing tech clients like Intel, Accenture and IBM, as well as non-tech ones such as Discovery Channel. My focus on tech deepened when I moved to Microland. At Brodeur, I worked again with companies like Cable & Wireless, Nortel and smaller tech firms. Infosys was also a key client in Europe for many years. I also developed expertise in structuring teams and building client programmes—skills I brought to Avian.

From the beginning, Nikhil and I made a conscious decision to be pioneers in innovation in the communications business. Our goal was to lead or, at the very least, be among the first to embrace new developments and drive change. This approach led us to establish several forward-thinking practices, including Chase India, a leading policy and advocacy firm shaping India's policy landscape, and EXPD (Experiential Digital and Content), our cutting-edge digital and content marketing service that keeps us at the forefront of the tech revolution. We were also early movers in launching a social impact practice and building one of the most robust data analytics teams in India. We went beyond the digital and leveraged insights in a broader sense to inform and guide our campaigns comprehensively.

Together, we led the firm for twelve glorious years, until we sold it to WE Communications in 2018. Today, the consultancy continues to thrive in its new form, with Nikhil as executive chair and me as group CEO. It's been a fascinating journey, where we've not only adapted to change but, in many cases, also driven it.

From all the campaigns I've worked on, crisis management has been my favourite. Whether it was handling the Tata crisis or more recent issues with start-ups, I personally stepped in, rolled up my sleeves and got on with the job. I love the challenge of turning around reputations or strengthening them under pressure. Managing the Godrej and Boyce split was another insightful experience.

Aside from campaigns, other milestones like landing our first major client or winning our first Consultancy of the

Year award in 2015 were deeply gratifying. That year was a turning point for us, especially when I was also recognised as the Global PR Leader of the Year by the International Communications Consultancy Organisation (ICCO).

When it comes to building and growing the firm, from Avian to Chase, and now with WE, where I have a broader APAC remit, my leadership style has always remained consistent. I would describe it as authentic, transparent, open and approachable. I believe in creating an environment where communication is clear, honest and straightforward. If you ask anyone who has worked with me, they would probably say I'm very approachable. My door is always open for everyone in the office—when we were a small firm and now with a larger operation with over 400 people.

I've evolved as a leader over time. Running a firm with five employees is very different from working with a team of five hundred. In the early days, I used to be more emotional when people left the company, but I've learnt that some things are inevitable—no matter what you do, you can't make everyone happy. I used to believe that it was my job to ensure everyone was satisfied, but it's impossible to please everyone.

Now I've shifted towards having a clear vision and ensuring that the people around me share it. Collaboration has become more critical than ever, and surrounding myself with the right people has made a significant difference. While I've grown personally and professionally, the core of my leadership—transparency, clarity, and collaboration—has always remained the same.

One thing I've been committed to throughout my career is giving back to the profession. Whether through my work with Public Relations Consultants Association of India (PRCAI) or the ICCO network globally, I've always made time to contribute. I served as chairperson, vice president and eventually president of PRCAI, spending about ten years helping build the association. It's great to see how well it's doing now. I also chair the Global Advisory Board for the Public Relations and Communications Association (PRCA), which allows me to contribute on a global scale. For me, it's essential to give back to the profession because it's our responsibility to ensure its growth. The best way to do that is through time and effort.

PR: A Multifaceted Strategic Function

Over the last twenty years, PR has evolved from a traditional media-focused discipline into a multifaceted strategic function that is now integral to business success. In the early 2000s, PR was largely centred around media relations—securing coverage in top-tier newspapers and prime-time news segments was the goal.

However, over the past decade, the significance of corporate reputation became increasingly apparent to CXOs. They realised that brands are defined not only by their products or services but also by their actions, values and public perception. Maintaining a strong reputation became a complex challenge, requiring expert guidance and tactical counsel. Smart brands quickly understood that investing in strategic PR and communications could make or break their business. This recognition elevated PR from a mere support function to a strategic imperative.

Today, PR professionals are tasked with addressing both commercial and societal challenges, with brand purpose now at the core of corporate reputation. Our 'Brands in Motion' study has shown that in a world filled with uncertainty, consumers expect brands to play a significant role in easing their anxieties and contributing to a better world. They demand authenticity and real impact. One of the most significant contributions PR firms have made is helping brands ensure that their chosen purpose is genuine and resonates deeply with consumers—whether through ESG initiatives, fostering diversity and inclusion or implementing better employee policies.

Global geopolitics has also emerged as a critical factor in shaping business and brand strategy. Political developments, trade policies and shifting alliances are now top of mind for businesses, as these factors can significantly impact operations, supply chains and reputations. PR and communications advisors have helped brands navigate these complexities with discretion and empathy. By exercising sensitivity and foresight, they have ensured that brands respond appropriately to geopolitical events, whether it's managing crises triggered by international conflicts or maintaining stakeholder trust during times of uncertainty.

Technology has further revolutionised PR, particularly with the rise of digital platforms. Digital PR has brought brands online, enabling real-time information sharing and interactive conversations with audiences. Social media platforms have democratised content creation, allowing immediate audience interaction. This shift required PR strategies to become more agile and proactive, using social media to shape narratives and build genuine connections. While traditional journalists and publications remain crucial for earned media, the rise of social media influencers has dramatically changed content distribution, fuelling the explosive growth of influencer marketing.

AI is the latest force driving change in PR, offering both opportunities and challenges. AI tools like chatbots and automated content creation are just the beginning. However, the adoption of AI comes with a responsibility to maintain transparency and ethical practices, ensuring that our use of these technologies builds trust rather than undermines it. Despite the growing influence of AI, human intelligence will remain paramount, guiding ethical decision-making and ensuring that our communications are both authentic and impactful.

The integration of advanced technology and data analytics has further transformed how we approach PR. By leveraging these tools, we can craft messages with pinpoint accuracy, ensuring our campaigns resonate deeply with target audiences. This tech-driven approach has turned PR professionals into storytellers, content creators and brand custodians. Our campaigns now seamlessly blend earned, owned and paid media, creating cohesive narratives that amplify our clients' voices.

The PR profession will continue to evolve. The rise of AI and other emerging technologies will further reshape our field. However, the core of what we do—building relationships, fostering trust and creating impactful stories—will remain unchanged. Our success will hinge on human intelligence and our capacity to adapt and innovate. The strength of our human connections and the people driving these efforts will always be at the core of what we do. By staying committed to authenticity and embracing new tools and strategies, we can ensure that PR continues to be a vital and dynamic force in the years to come.

15

Anurag Mittal

Founder, NewsVoir

'The journey from my early days to where I am now has been deeply fulfilling, shaped by incredible opportunities, challenges and the relationships I've built along the way.'

Leading India's News Wire Surge

I was born in 1973 in Delhi, and grew up in a close-knit, traditional family, living with my grandparents and other senior family members. Our household was deeply rooted in values, discipline and a sense of purpose, which became the cornerstone of my upbringing.

Having my grandparents around was a blessing. Their storytelling—whether about the Mahabharata, Ramayana or other mythological tales—not only entertained but also instilled moral lessons and a sense of cultural identity that laid a strong foundation for my outlook on life.

My father, a lawyer, chose a professional path despite belonging to a family of businesspeople. Even today, he continues to work with dedication. My younger sister, Ruchira, followed in his footsteps and became a corporate lawyer. My mother, a homemaker, was the true pillar of our household—a strong and resolute woman who nurtured us with her unwavering strength and wisdom.

I had a happy childhood, filled with learning and meaningful interactions with family, extended relatives and peers. I attended Delhi Public School, Mathura Road, where I built lasting friendships. Being part of an extended family meant I also shared a lot of time with cousins.

Sports were a significant part of my early years. I played cricket at both school and college levels. I also dabbled in other sports, which taught me about teamwork and healthy competition—qualities that have stayed with me throughout life.

After completing school, I pursued a bachelor's degree in economics at Hansraj College, Delhi University. Those years were transformative, as I balanced academics with playing cricket. While economics was a demanding subject, I gained exposure to business by joining the office of an extended family member who was a well-known exporter.

At seventeen, I began spending a few hours daily at his office after college. This experience introduced me to the nuances of international trade and the fundamentals of business.

After completing my undergraduate studies, I pursued an LLB degree from the Faculty of Law at Delhi University. Coming from a family of lawyers, it seemed like a natural choice. Although I was initially hesitant about a career in law, I decided to explore it.

After completing my law degree, I decided to take a break from academics and began working. It was during this period that I soon realised law wasn't my calling. Instead, I wanted to either become a working professional or eventually start a venture of my own.

To build a foundation for this vision, I pursued an MBA degree at the International Management Institute (IMI) in New Delhi. It was an enriching experience that provided not only academic insights but also opportunities for valuable interactions with fellow students and professors, some of whom even served as advisors to the Government of India. The camaraderie and intellectual exchange at IMI were exceptional, making it a transformative chapter of my life.

The skills and knowledge I gained during those two years, combined with the practical insights from my law degree, equipped me well for the professional world. I leveraged my experience in the exports and manufacturing sectors and joined a company that specialised in the publishing and printing of high-quality books.

This role proved to be a pivotal experience. In my early twenties, the company entrusted me with significant responsibilities, including representing the marketing and exports team internationally. I travelled extensively, often three to four times a year, to various countries. The exposure to international business and the manufacturing process, and collaborations with prominent business leaders was invaluable.

Later, I received an exciting opportunity to work in the US with a tech company from a co-traveller to the US. They offered me a position, and my H1B visa was processed. However, around this time, my mother's health began to deteriorate, and I made the difficult decision to return to India to be with her. I chose to stay back, ultimately surrendering my visa and letting go of the US opportunity. This decision marked a turning point, and by the early 2000s, I had firmly planted myself back in India, ready to embrace the next chapter of my life and career.

When I returned to India, the dot-com boom was at its peak, and I joined a job site. At the time, working for a tech company came with a certain allure. People believed that anyone associated with the dot-com world was on the brink of becoming a multimillionaire. The industry was buzzing with excitement, and I felt like I was part of something revolutionary.

Our office was a dynamic mix of talent, with over fifty people from diverse backgrounds, including professionals from Microsoft, IITs and IIMs. It was an environment filled with energy and promise. The company culture was vibrant, with pizza parties, bowling nights, go-karting and endless discussions about funding rounds and valuations. It seemed like nothing could go wrong.

The founders were heavily investing in the company, and there was a palpable sense of optimism as we prepared for our first round of funding. I vividly remember a meeting in Mumbai where everything seemed to align, and we were confident the funding would come through within weeks. But then, the bubble burst.

In a matter of weeks, everything changed. The funding never materialised, and the dot-com crash hit us hard. From a team of over fifty, we shrank to eight to ten people. Many of my colleagues, including senior professionals with hefty pay packages, either resigned or were let go. I was heading business development at the time, but with the team reduced to a fraction of its size, I was tasked with keeping the company afloat.

Suddenly, the lavish lifestyle disappeared. Office expenses were slashed to the extent that even tea was rationed. Our once-grand vision had to be reevaluated as we pivoted from being a job site to functioning more like a recruitment agency, focusing on offline services to sustain operations. Those of us who remained gave our all to keep the company running and retain clients organically.

The experience was humbling and taught me invaluable lessons. One was the critical importance of having a returning client base. Projections and Excel sheet profits may look promising, but they mean little without steady cash flow and profitability.

Another was the value of nurturing relationships with vendors. During our toughest times, some vendors stood by us, continuing to provide services despite delayed payments. Their support highlighted the importance of maintaining strong partnerships with all stakeholders in a business ecosystem.

These lessons have always stayed with me. The dot-com experience taught me resilience, resourcefulness, and the significance of building a sustainable and relationship-driven business.

The job site had pivoted into a recruitment agency, and I realised it wasn't aligned with my goals and expectations. While exploring new digital opportunities, I got the chance to work as a digital consultant for one of the leading PR firms, IPAN, a WPP Group firm.

There I collaborated with a small team to create an innovative online platform called Business to Media. It was designed to publish and distribute corporate news, a groundbreaking concept at the time. We identified similar business models globally and decided to collaborate with companies like Business Wire in the US. This partnership eventually led us to adopt the Business Wire brand name in India. Business Wire India became the country's first corporate newswire service.

Launching the wire service was a major milestone, but it required significant effort to educate stakeholders about its value. We engaged with large news agencies, online publications, PR firms and corporates to demonstrate how this platform could benefit their outreach and communication strategies. We also organised breakfast meetings, roundtable discussions and workshops with editors, journalists and corporate representatives. It was great to watch the ecosystem gradually embrace this new model.

Along with this, I was also entrusted with leading a media monitoring unit within the WPP Group. At the time, the process was entirely offline—manually reading newspapers, cutting and pasting clippings and sharing them with clients. I worked on digitising the entire workflow. We also evaluated several requests for proposal and eventually partnered with a large tech company to implement a state-of-the-art solution.

This transformation involved deploying scanners to digitise newspapers and leveraging optical character recognition technology to extract relevant news clippings using keywords. The automation streamlined operations, reducing manual effort and improving efficiency. It was a significant investment with a gestation period, but the WPP management trusted our vision. Within a few years, the business broke even and started delivering real-time tracking and analytics to clients.

We also developed a dashboarding solution to provide clients with real-time coverage updates. Our clientele included notable organisations like UNICEF and Reliance Communications. For Reliance, we tracked media coverage across fifty cities, including managing negative reportage during new service launches. For UNICEF, we monitored their critical polio vaccination campaign to ensure its visibility and impact in the media.

This dual experience—building Business Wire India and digitising the media monitoring business—was immensely enriching. Over twelve years as a consultant with WPP, I gained exposure to cutting-edge solutions, worked with prestigious clients and witnessed the transformation of traditional processes into efficient digital ecosystems.

After this remarkable journey, I felt the calling to venture into something of my own. I partnered with a friend to create a boutique hotel property in the Himalayan hills. We had acquired some land and began constructing a boutique property in Mukteshwar near Nainital. Mukteshwar is a stunning place, and our property was strategically located to offer breathtaking views of the valley and snow-clad peaks. As we started building, I noticed a gap in the market that could potentially be addressed.

While overseeing the development, I continued working as a digital consultant, advising clients on international outreach, engagement strategies, search engine optimisation and content distribution. One thing led to another and NewsVoir was founded in 2014.

Some of my friends from PR consultancies suggested that we could join forces with a larger group, with the potential for an acquisition. However, with all humility, I declined the offer at the time. I was just starting this venture, uncertain of where it would lead, and I wanted to run it independently without external funding or partnerships. I aimed to experiment with a new model.

Unlike traditional news distribution companies like Business Wire, which relied heavily on technology for content dissemination, we developed a blended model at NewsVoir. This approach combined the efficiency of technology with strong media relations. We explained to journalists and editors the nuances of the news we were distributing and how it could benefit both the media and our clients. This personalised approach, paired with innovative technological tools, worked exceptionally well for us.

On the technology front, we implemented unique features that ensured the news we distributed was well-indexed in the online space, especially on search engines like Google. This significantly boosted visibility and impact for our clients. By blending technology with personal engagement, we created a distinctive offering in the market.

Over time, the business matured and began to operate almost on autopilot, requiring only minimal supervision. This gave me more free time for collaboration opportunities with old friends and clients. Balancing the creation of a boutique property and building an innovative venture like NewsVoir was a fulfilling journey.

I am grateful for the trust and support I received from friends and well-wishers working in corporates and PR firms. As a new entrant in the market, their willingness to give us a chance was invaluable. I'm proud to say that in most cases, we delivered on their trust, which led to returning and repeat customers for us. This loyalty kept us going and motivated us to strive for excellence.

We had begun to see significant growth in both domestic and international markets. We now have our own distribution network in the Middle East and we're also actively building our presence in the US and already manage substantial distribution activities globally.

We are also constantly looking to leverage cloud-based SaaS tools to better address the evolving needs of PR and corporate communication professionals. These tools are designed to add more value and create innovative solutions for our clients.

Throughout this journey, we have remained true to our vision—adding value, being helpful, and fostering meaningful relationships. Whether it's with clients, vendors, or partners, these associations form the foundation of everything we do.

The journey from my early days to where I am now has been deeply fulfilling, shaped by incredible opportunities, challenges and the relationships I've built along the way.

Evolution on the Back of Digital Transformation

PR has shifted from relying solely on traditional press releases and media coverage to leveraging digital platforms, social media and online news portals. The rise of search engine optimisation (SEO) and content marketing has transformed how PR professionals craft their messages to ensure maximum online visibility and discoverability. The business has seen some remarkable changes.

The evolution of press releases: Press releases have undergone a dramatic transformation. In the early 2000s, they were often physically delivered or sent as email attachments with plain text. Today, they have evolved into 'smart releases', enriched with embedded links, images, infographics and videos. These enhancements make them powerful tools of digital PR, helping organisations achieve better indexing on search engines and driving more dynamic engagement with online audiences.

Modern press releases not only communicate news but also bolster a brand's online presence, as they often remain accessible indefinitely, contributing to search engine rankings and SEO efforts.

Real-time engagement: With the advent of social media, brands are now expected to respond to crises, customer queries and trends almost instantaneously, with delays often leading to reputational damage. Social media platforms like X have become key battlegrounds for real-time PR strategies.

Data-driven strategies: PR is no longer a guessing game. Analytics tools that gauge metrics such as reach, engagement, impressions and sentiment analysis now allow professionals to measure campaign success with precision.

Integration with marketing: PR and marketing have become more integrated than ever before. Campaigns are now designed to support lead generation, sales goals and brand awareness simultaneously. Integrated marketing communication ensures consistent messaging across paid, earned, shared and owned media.

The rise of influencer relations: The PR landscape has expanded to include influencers, bloggers and content creators as they often yield higher engagement than traditional media coverage. Influencers are now considered vital partners in PR campaigns, as they have direct access to highly engaged niche audiences. Collaborations with influencers often yield higher engagement than traditional media coverage.

Audience-centric messaging: Gone are the days of one-size-fits-all messages. Modern PR focuses on creating audience-specific messaging, keeping in mind different demographics, interests and geographies that resonate on an emotional level.

Emphasis on transparency and authenticity: Consumers today demand transparency and authenticity from brands. PR campaigns prioritise ethical storytelling, open communication and trust-building, as any perception of dishonesty can spread rapidly online and harm reputations.

The role of crisis management: With the 24/7 news cycle and social media's influence, crises can escalate within hours.

Brands must now invest in proactive crisis preparedness and real-time response strategies to safeguard their reputations.

Shift from print to digital media: The decline of traditional print media and the growth of digital platforms have fundamentally changed PR outreach strategies. Online publications, blogs and news aggregators have become critical for securing media coverage and achieving global reach.

Technological advancements: Technologies like AI, automation and virtual platforms have revolutionised PR because they streamline media monitoring and sentiment analysis, while virtual events and webinars have replaced traditional press conferences, particularly since the COVID-19 pandemic.

Global reach and localisation: Digital platforms have given PR campaigns a global reach, allowing brands to connect with international audiences. Simultaneously, there's a growing focus on localisation, tailoring messages to regional audiences while respecting cultural nuances.

Focus on sustainability and CSR: Companies actively highlight their sustainability and outreach efforts and their stance on social issues to align with stakeholder expectations and build goodwill.

The decline of gatekeeping: Traditional media outlets once acted as gatekeepers to brand narratives, but digital transformation has empowered companies to take control of their storytelling. Blogs, social media platforms and owned content channels allow brands to connect directly with their audiences without relying solely on third-party validation.

The importance of reputation management: In the digital age, the internet's permanent memory has made reputation management a core function of PR. Brands now invest in monitoring and managing their digital footprints to ensure that positive narratives outweigh any potential negative content.

Evolving media relationships: While relationships with journalists remain important, the nature of these interactions has shifted. Email pitches, social media DMs and other digital channels have replaced traditional phone calls and in-person meetings. Building strong media relationships today requires a mix of personalisation, relevance, and digital savvy.

Over the past two decades, PR has dramatically shifted from traditional methodologies to a digital-centric approach. Our platform harnesses the power of advanced digital technologies to facilitate real-time interactions and implement strategic, data-driven campaigns. Committed to innovation, NewsVoir stays at the forefront of PR trends, helping shape public perceptions and strengthen brand value in a dynamic global market.

16

Abhilasha Padhy

Co-Founder and Joint Managing Director, 80 db Communications

'While I take immense pride in the success stories of our clients, our success is driven by a highly capable team.'

From a Childhood in PSU Townships to the Big City Life of Brand and Marketing

I was born in Berhampur, Odisha, but my childhood was spent across various places—Bihar, Haldia, Gujarat and Panipat—because of my father's transferable job as an engineer with Indian Oil. I attended seven schools during this time, growing up in the sanitised environments of PSU townships. I completed my schooling in Panipat before moving to Delhi for higher studies.

I pursued English literature at St Stephen's College, Delhi University, and later went on to secure a master's degree in mass communication from Symbiosis, where I opted for the integrated communications course that had a mix of advertising and PR. This decision, made with the guidance and support of my parents, marked the beginning of a journey that would eventually lead me to PR instead of my original aspiration of journalism.

Despite growing up in a technocrat household, there was never any undue pressure to pursue science. By the mid-1990s, it was clear I would choose humanities, a decision my family fully supported.

My first internship was with Corporate Voice Weber Shandwick in Mumbai, where I worked with Aparna Thomas's team on the McDonald's crisis, where the brand was accused of adding beef to its products. As an intern, my role primarily involved collecting clippings, note-taking and observing the meticulous management of brand reputation. That experience inspired my interest in PR, and I decided to pivot from journalism to this field.

I began my career at Integral PR in Mumbai, working on lifestyle clients like Bacardi during its heyday of high-profile events and parties. However, after eight months, I returned to Delhi due to the high cost of living in Mumbai and joined Genesis PR in Gurgaon. There, I worked in the corporate team, handling B2B tech clients like Navision, which is now a part of Microsoft.

I spent around five transformative years with 2020 Media, which truly shaped my career and personal growth. I worked on some of my best clients, built lifelong relationships and found both my future co-founder and my mentor.

I handled prominent accounts like Canon, Samsung, Deloitte and Citrix, gaining experience across consumer tech and B2B tech. After leaving 2020 Media, I had a brief corporate stint with Mercer and Philips before taking a two-year maternity break in 2010–2011.

At that time, I reconnected with Kiran Ray Chaudhury, my mentor at 2020 Media. She was running her first start-up, Aether Marketing, and we began collaborating on projects. Since I worked as an independent consultant, this period allowed me to explore the potential of working independently, securing clients and executing projects single-handedly. Although I eventually returned to the workforce with Google, the idea of starting something of my own had begun to take root.

By 2014–2015, when start-ups were creating a buzz in India, Kiran and I decided to launch 80 dB. Our discussions turned into action when an acquaintance approached us and insisted we work on their brand. This became our first client and the catalyst for registering the company. Within a few months, we had signed fifteen clients, necessitating office space, a team and the formal establishment of 80 dB.

Interestingly, our first client had an innovative concept, albeit slightly ahead of its time for India. They offered a private 911-like emergency service. For instance, if you had a car breakdown or a personal emergency, they would dispatch a team to assist you until official help arrived. Their 'feet-on-street' model catered to various situations—whether unlocking a stuck door, helping with a gas issue or providing roadside assistance.

From these beginnings, 80 dB grew rapidly. We've learnt over the last five-odd years that any communications strategy must integrate social and owned platforms, tailored to the client's needs. Social media, thought leadership, influencer outreach and engagement with key opinion leaders have become essential components of our work.

One of the standout clients in our portfolio is Agnikul Cosmos, an aerospace company incubated at IIT-Madras and supported by a VC we collaborate with. Agnikul specialises in creating customisable, transportable launch vehicles for small satellites, branded as Agnibaan. In 2023, they made history by unveiling a single-piece 3D-printed engine, which can be manufactured in just seventy-two hours without human intervention. This milestone was not only significant for Agnikul but also for us as we worked closely with the ISRO team during this historic launch. While our lead team was on-site, it was an incredibly proud moment to contribute to such groundbreaking innovation.

We also work extensively with new-age businesses and start-ups, including those in the deep tech, space tech and health sectors. For example, we collaborate with W Health Ventures, which focuses on tackling modern lifestyle diseases like diabetes, obesity and pain management. These issues have immense market potential in the US, but awareness in India is still growing.

Another significant client is Jagatjit Industries, the parent company of Aristocrat Whiskey. They were among our early clients, starting in 2015. Our partnership focused on positioning Roshni Sanah Jaiswal, a third-generation entrepreneur, as the company's restructuring officer. At the time, Jagatjit's market share was declining. We supported Roshni in raising funds, enhancing the company's perception and revamping their annual reports. Through these efforts, we witnessed a tangible impact, with improvements in the company's performance on the stock market.

While I take immense pride in the success stories of our clients, our success is driven by a highly capable team. They handle day-to-day client interactions and operations, ensuring that each project receives the attention it deserves. For instance, I may celebrate Agnikul's achievements, but the credit for their operational excellence goes entirely to my team.

Building and Nurturing Brand Reputation

I've been in the profession for over twenty years now, and I've watched the landscape evolve faster in the last few years than when PR first became an essential tool of branding in the twentieth century. This is owing, in no small part, to the explosion of newer digital platforms—especially its growth from a personal space to one where businesses broadcast what they stand for to the world. PR firms are no longer restricted to their traditional role, and digital platforms are enabling firms to take on a more integrated approach. They have ventured into different areas such as social media and digital marketing, video and content development and much more. It has been a great opportunity for firms to innovate, open up new streams of revenue and differentiate themselves from competition.

Increasing spends on technology and enhancing capabilities by adding social, digital and data to their traditional offerings are necessary to ensure the emerging and evolving communication needs of clients in a dynamic environment. In an era of information overload and fake news, a mix of technology and human endeavour will provide a solid foundation to sustain and strengthen clients' reputations.

The C-suite's reliance on PR has also grown. Now, more than ever, business leaders in India understand the value of PR in sculpting both their corporate and personal narratives.

Lastly, the global political landscape has left its mark on PR. We've had to adapt and become nimble, moving beyond traditional methods to offer integrated services that can swiftly respond to geopolitical changes. This adaptability has become a cornerstone of our work, enabling us to navigate the complexities of today's global environment effectively.

17

Pooja Pathak

Co-Founder, Media Mantra

'If you enjoy your work, you'll find a way to make it a priority.'

From a Not-for-profit to Public Relations

I WAS BORN IN AHMEDABAD, BUT I ONLY LIVED THERE FOR A short while. My roots are in the Delhi NCR region, where I've spent the majority of my life. My parents have greatly influenced my path. Both of my parents were working professionals; hence education has always been non-negotiable in our home. My father works in the corporate field while also pursuing teaching in colleges and universities, while my mother is currently a school principal. My sister is also in the communications field and briefly taught in a college as well. This strong educational foundation has shaped my approach to life and my career.

My sister and I were always encouraged to take independent decisions, though with guidance from our parents. My greatest lesson is to be fearless in pursuing my dreams and to never let my aspirations be stifled. These helped me immensely when I co-founded Media Mantra. I think I had an entrepreneurial streak even in college when I took on freelance work for lifestyle companies, building websites and writing extensively for them.

I did my schooling at Amity, Noida, followed by graduation from Miranda House, Delhi University. I have always loved writing, and at Miranda House I was actively involved in the creative writing society, and eventually became the president in my final year, which sparked my interest in exploring PR as a career. I thrived in environments where I could express myself. I learnt that about myself in school when I became the prefect. Academics weren't always my main focus, but I've always valued meaningful conversations and learning from others.

After my undergraduate studies, I worked for about a year and a half with Planman Consulting in their PR department. I soon moved to Sydney, Australia, for a master's degree and worked there for a while as well. I opted for a post-graduate degree in community development because I wanted to work in an NGO. That's how I got the opportunity to work with United Nations Youth on an intriguing project about Copenhagen's climate.

In Australia, I explored various avenues, particularly in writing. I contributed articles to *Indian Link*, a local Indian organisation, and had a gig as a radio jockey (RJ) for about a year and a half. My experience as an RJ enhanced my critical thinking and broadened my perspective in many ways. I also worked with several Australian companies, gaining valuable insights into how businesses operate there. I was deeply inspired by their work culture and style of functioning. At that time, I had two career paths in mind: either to continue in the NGO sector or explore PR. I noticed an overlap between communication and community development, which drew me to PR. It seemed like a natural fit. But back then, PR wasn't well understood. Many people assumed it wasn't a viable career path and would eventually lead to advertising. But I was firm—if I was choosing PR, why would I switch to advertising?

I returned to India to visit family and reassess whether I could settle in India. If not, my plan was to return to Australia. Unsure of what to do, I applied to and was offered a job at Value 360, where I met my husband Udit. This encounter changed everything. Soon, we fell in love, got married and started planning for a family.

When Udit first mentioned starting Media Mantra, I was hesitant. I do not have a high risk appetite, and we had just become parents. The thought of both of us leaving stable jobs to start a business felt daunting.

However, I'm so glad I trusted Udit and didn't let my fears take over. Some things are just destined to happen, and Media Mantra was one of them. We took the plunge, and here we are today.

Starting Media Mantra coincided with a major personal milestone—becoming a mother. Balancing both roles has been challenging, but my parents' unwavering belief in education and independence has been a constant source of strength.

Interestingly, I never formally studied communication. At Miranda House, I pursued philosophy honours, and communication wasn't a part of my curriculum even in my post-graduate studies. However, life took an interesting turn, and now I find myself teaching communication and PR in colleges. I truly enjoy it.

When we started Media Mantra, someone recommended me to give a guest lecture at the Indian Institute of Learning and Advanced Development, which had also recently launched. I was thrilled and put a lot of effort into preparing for it. The response from students was positive, and I was later invited to teach regularly. I began teaching elements of PR to PGDM students, and eventually post-graduate students as well. I taught for five or six years, and the first employees we hired at Media Mantra were actually some of my students.

We gave them pre-placement offers, and many of them stayed with us for a long time. Teaching became a passion. This is the perfect example of how passion can sometimes take you places that education alone can't.

While building Media Mantra, my experience as a mother brought a unique perspective that I don't think any other role could offer. Motherhood brings with it emotions and responsibilities that shape you in ways you can't predict, and I found that creating the right support system was essential. Such a network of support can help you thrive in both personal and professional spaces.

Through this journey, I also discovered a lot about myself. What I once saw as my strengths shifted over time, and I had to change. I am a highly adaptable person, and that has helped me evolve with the changing demands of both my personal and professional life. In doing so, I've learnt that I contribute best when I feel deeply connected to the people and environment around me.

The office is my personal space, where I truly feel at home. Despite being a mother and a wife, the office gives me a distinct sense of fulfilment and joy. I look forward to going to work every day because I've built it from the ground up, much like raising a child. The sentimental attachment I have to

Media Mantra is deep, and it brings me immense pride to see the company grow.

My aim is to keep the office energy positive and vibrant. We have a small temple here, and often, I come in early to perform my *pujas and havans*. It's a unique side of corporate life, but it grounds me and gives me strength. And I believe this sense of calm and positivity spreads to everyone who is part of the Media Mantra family.

The softer aspects of life—values, relationships and spirituality—matter a great deal. Of course, business goals, competition and chasing targets are important, but there's more to life than that. Our company is called Media Mantra for a reason. We are rooted in the Indian PR profession, and maintaining that connection to our origins is crucial. We all come from humble beginnings, and I'm deeply grateful for how far we've come.

There's not a single day when I look back with regret or complaints. As long as we continue running this company, my dream is for Media Mantra to remain a place that thrives on positive energy and growth.

When you're truly committed—no matter what role you play—you find a way to balance everything. Whether it was taking my child on playdates or organising his birthday parties, I made sure I never missed anything important. Weekends became the time to catch up if I missed something during the week.

If something needed extra effort, I'd stretch myself to get it done, and I'm okay with that. I'm not doing anything extraordinary; many people are doing it, some even more. But if you're happy with what you're doing, that's what matters most. No regrets—just a sense of fulfilment.

As a woman, I've realised that people will take your career as seriously as you do. The moment you stop prioritising it, everyone else will follow suit. It's not just about financial contribution or external expectations. If you enjoy your work, you'll find a way to make it a priority. I look forward to work. I don't need to be pushed into it. In fact, I'd encourage others to find their passion and pursue it relentlessly.

So, my advice to women, especially those in the workforce, is to be clear about what you want. Once you figure that out, don't let anything stop you. Even motherhood doesn't mean you have to put your career on hold—you can do both if you want to, and it's entirely possible to find that balance.

If you want to juggle multiple tasks simultaneously, you need to be extra passionate about each one of them. That passion is what drives you forward. Education is important—foundational learning is essential—but when you genuinely love what you do, it brings out a certain authenticity in your words and actions. People can sense the truth in what you're saying, and that builds trust.

We all have things that can either pull us down or lift us up—it's up to us to decide which direction we want to go. I've always focused on the things that uplift me, and that has been key to my mindset. Writing has always been my most treasured skill. Whether it was writing daily press pieces or working on projects, I found it exciting to see how many words I could churn out, and that passion fuelled me.

On Media Mantra's roster are some incredible campaigns. But we're not just about them; it's the milestones we've achieved as a company that are more memorable. The first time Media Mantra started winning awards was pivotal, and it felt just as thrilling as any major campaign. We were learning how to write award entries, understand the process and grow together as an organisation. Starting the company when I was just twenty-six, twelve years ago, so much of what we've learnt, unlearnt and experienced comes directly from building Media Mantra.

In terms of leadership, I've changed drastically from how I started to where I am now. Leadership evolves as you change as a person. I never want to be consistent in one style because that would make me feel stagnant. However, one thing that has remained constant over the years is our drive. Udit and I have always been aggressive and dedicated to our work, and that has never wavered. We've never been the type to check the clock and head home; we genuinely enjoy the work we do.

PR isn't just our profession; it's woven into every part of our lives, both professional and personal. That's the kind of passion that fuels us, and it sets us apart.

One of the most important grounding aspects of my life is spirituality. I hold it very dear because it centres my entire being. I tend to overthink, and I love engaging in deep conversations and reflective practices, and going to mindfulness retreats. But I've realised that sometimes, the answers we seek don't come from practical knowledge; they require a spiritual understanding. Spirituality opens doors within us that we didn't even know existed. Finding that 'hook'—that inner anchor—is essential.

Life will always present challenges—it's inevitable. But the most important ecosystem we need to nurture is the one within ourselves. If you can develop the right inner ecosystem, with the right guidance from the right people, the external factors won't matter. Spirituality is more about meditation and healing. I'm fortunate to have a living guru who guides me, and I follow a small circle of people who help shape my spiritual journey. It has become a regular practice, and over the years it has enriched my life. Spirituality is very different from religion. We can integrate it into our daily lives, even while working or managing other responsibilities. It is a practical solution to life. It provides a framework for mindfulness and self-awareness, and I think everyone should have their own 'lookbook' for life—a guide to staying centred and grounded amidst everything else.

It's essential to have the right tribe of people in your life—those who will support you unconditionally. You don't need a large circle, just a few individuals who are there for you when it counts. Second, it's important to have unfiltered, non-judgmental conversations with someone you trust. It might be one or two people, but that's enough. You don't need more than that to feel heard and understood. Third, you must know your own strengths and weaknesses. We live in a world of endless options at our fingertips, but what matters most is knowing what resonates with you personally. That self-awareness is crucial. And lastly, it's okay to stand alone in your beliefs. What's important is to be truthful, loyal and honest to yourself and others. I strongly believe in honesty—despite everything, I still think the world isn't as bad as it's often portrayed. There are still good people and things worth trusting.

The world today is divided into two parallels: the chaos of 'this happened, that happened' and another path where trust and honesty prevail. I believe we should choose the latter, working together to create a better ecosystem. That's how we can shape a better future for ourselves and those around us.

The Transformation of Public Relations

The landscape of public relations has undergone a profound change, evolving from traditional media relations to an integrated, multi-channel discipline shaped by digital advancements. From covering just print media in the olden days, with the advent of the internet, social networking and mobile technology, PR has progressed into another dimension. In today's time, it not only includes media coverage but also reputation management, the development of credibility and strategic business goals centred toward harmonious organisational objectives.

At the core of modern PR is the realisation that brands need to establish credibility through authentic, transparent communication. For the modern practitioner of PR, the challenge is telling an influencing story to the target audience and establishing brand credibility. No longer are media placements the end-all; rather, the outcome of investment is indeed to stimulate brand loyalty, customer engagement and long-term reputation management. This strategic role has stretched the activities of PR from the old publicity-oriented approach to a more sophisticated output-oriented model.

Digital has undeniably been the shift, with the global PR market projected to grow exponentially. This reflects how brands care more about PR as an integral part of their communication strategies. The introduction of AI and data analytics has brought about another revolutionary change in the profession. With AI, the PR business can now automate media monitoring, sentiment analysis and even crisis detection, allowing PR professionals to react correctly to real-time developments. Data-driven insights have also become vital, and are now used in tailoring the firm's approach according to audience behaviour, business trends and campaign performance metrics.

Today's PR programmes are holistic because they deal with multiple platforms; the three nets of earned, owned and paid media are being amalgamated today to deliver a single brand message. Whether a crisis, product launch or establishing thought leadership, the approach today gets integrated by the collaboration of digital marketers, content creators and social media managers.

As PR continues to evolve in this digital-first world, keeping pace with the latest technological progress and readjusting according to the fast-changing horizon is now extremely important. As there is an increasing tendency to view the world digitally, it is very crucial for PR consultancies to go beyond just reporting media coverage and to promise full-spectrum solutions that enhance their client's reputation while encouraging meaningful engagement.

18

Udit Pathak

Co-Founder, Media Mantra

'Sometimes it's not about running an elaborate campaign—it's about that one impactful story that can create the buzz and build awareness that a client needs.'

From a Traditional Family Business to a PR Enterprise

I was born and raised in Gurgaon, and completed my schooling there at Bluebells Model Senior Secondary School. My family has a business background, and my father and grandparents migrated from Punjab to Gurgaon in the 1960s to set up a factory. Back then, Gurgaon was vastly different from what it is today—just open land before a few businesses started to emerge. My grandfather used to tell stories about how they arrived with barely a rupee or two, and from those humble beginnings, our family worked hard to build something significant.

We established a successful factory that became the largest manufacturer of crockery in India. We introduced stoneware crockery to the country, and I vividly remember seeing our company's name in my commerce textbooks. The entire family was involved—my father, his cousins, my uncle—all working together in what was a classic joint family business, which was quite common in those days.

After our success with crockery, my father and uncle ventured into the shoe business during the 1980s and 1990s. They secured distribution deals with well-known brands like Bata and Phoenix International and became one of the biggest distributors in Haryana. Our family had always aimed to excel in everything we did, and fortunately, we were able to achieve that.

However, things started to take a turn when my grandmother was diagnosed with cancer in the early 2000s. Around the same time, Chinese manufacturing began to penetrate India, flooding it with cheaper goods, which severely affected our business. Government policies seemed to favour these imports, and we struggled to compete.

Moreover, constant changes in manufacturing regulations—shifting from coal to diesel, then to LPG and later to CNG—put a huge financial strain on us. Our factory was entirely self-funded, with no external investors, so every time the policies shifted, we had to go back to the market to raise funds. You can do that once or twice, but not every few years. Eventually, the mounting debts made it clear that continuing wasn't sustainable.

We collectively decided it was best to close the factory rather than sink more money into it. Preserving the land we owned seemed like the wiser decision. After we shut down the factory, I ventured into the workforce after studying mass communication from Guru Jambeshwar University.

My mother played a crucial role in my early journey. She was always the one to insist that I get a job first. She felt that the lessons I would learn from a job would be completely different from what I would experience in business, especially if I joined my father's company.

My first job was at Aaj Tak with Headlines Today as a guest coordinator. I've always had an entrepreneurial spirit, whether it was in PR, the crockery business or something else entirely. When I was working at Aaj Tak, I even thought about starting my own channel one day.

However, since I was only in my early twenties at the time, I didn't have the full picture. Our exposure to the world was quite limited, and technology wasn't as advanced as it is today. The start-up culture in India was just beginning to emerge, around 2004–2006, and there weren't as many opportunities or resources available.

Eventually, I realised that starting a channel would require much more than just funding. So, I shifted my focus and considered reopening our family's crockery factory. Around that time, I spoke to my cousin, Amish Devgan, who is now a well-known media personality and an editor at Network18. He helped me land a job at Value 360, and that's when my journey in public relations truly began. It's also where I met Pooja, who went on to become my co-founder and wife.

I developed a real passion for PR, especially because it was all about building connections and relationships. Back then, PR was more focused on press releases and getting stories out rather than brand creation. But over time, I came to understand the true power of PR. Given my entrepreneurial mindset, I was clear from day one at Value 360 that I would either give my all to this job or start my own business.

Pooja had no plans to start a business, but I kept encouraging and trying to persuade her. Thanks to my PR skills, I was able to convince her, and she eventually agreed to partner with me. Together, we founded Media Mantra in 2012.

Coincidentally, our son Yuvan was born the day we made the decision. That day, both Pooja and I resigned from our jobs and committed fully to the business. Looking back, I knew that if I hadn't taken the leap then, I would have regretted it in five years. So 26 August 2012 happens to be my firm's and son's birthday.

We were fortunate that clients came on board without much difficulty. Within the first two to three months, we became profitable and began hiring colleagues.

One of our key advantages was that Pooja excelled at media relations, securing coverage and getting stories out, while I focused on bringing in new business. My strong media connections from my previous job also played a significant role in helping us grow. As a result, we quickly became a force to be reckoned with, steadily winning accounts and expanding our team.

Our first client was DeliveryOnCall.com. Interestingly, they had the same concept that today's quick commerce companies offer. Back in 2012, the founder had the vision to offer rapid deliveries, just like today's ten- to twenty-minute delivery services.

He even bought a hundred motorcycles and successfully implemented the delivery model in Noida. However, despite the early success, he couldn't secure more funding. He wasn't able to raise the capital needed from VCs, and had to shut down the business. But the vision he had back then was ahead of its time.

Despite not having any external funding or investments, we managed to secure him a half-page feature in *The Economic*

Times, which turned into a very successful campaign for us. After that story, many companies started approaching us, impressed by the fact that we could get a non-funded start-up featured in a major newspaper. It became a strong testament to our media relations capabilities.

After DeliveryOnCall.com, we brought in more clients, such as IndiaReads.com, an online library founded by Gunjan Vedha, who also consulted with the Planning Commission of India. Our third client was Planman Consulting's HR division, Planman HR.

We also signed Executive Access, one of Asia's largest executive search firms, which is still a client today. As we kept winning accounts, we built a strong reputation in the HR domain, bringing on clients like Unison International, a recruitment company based in Gurgaon. Our first five clients played a critical role in establishing our credibility and driving our growth forward.

We were working across multiple industries, handling a diverse range of clients—from start-ups and technology companies to HR firms and education. We also landed major accounts like Akash Institute and Seniorworld.com, which focused on serving the elderly population. Seniorworld launched a phone specifically designed for seniors, and since they were a start-up with no external funding, it was a huge deal. However, for the media, it was just another company trying to stand out. To change that, we got NDTV's Rajiv Makhni to review the phone, and he gave it a glowing, unpaid review, long before influencer marketing was the norm. That review brought Seniorworld significant downloads and orders, and the client was thrilled with the outcome. From then on, despite the growing competition and bigger agencies approaching them, they stayed with us.

This experience taught me that sometimes it's not about running an elaborate campaign—it's about that one impactful story that can create the buzz and build the awareness that a client needs.

Another standout moment was when I personally worked on a story about the business model of executive search firms. It was a B2B feature, and I got four of my clients featured in a half-page national story in *The Economic Times*, with no other competitors mentioned. That remains one of my proudest achievements, and I still have the clipping.

The only way to succeed in business is to show your work, and that only happens when you're actively implementing the solutions you propose to clients. When we first started out, Pooja and I would come to the office dressed in formals, even though it was just the two of us and a peon. We maintained a disciplined routine—arriving by 10.00 a.m. and breaking for lunch at 1.30 p.m. Every time we received some money, Pooja would head downstairs to buy something for our child. These were the small joys that kept us going.

Our initial focus was on earning enough to support our growing family, but over time, we shifted towards building an organisation that could stand the test of time.

When it comes to leadership, I consider myself an aggressive and bold leader. Some might view aggressive as a negative term, but it's about taking bold steps and moving forward. Of course, not every decision is perfect, but I'm okay with that because bold moves are necessary for growth. One of my bravest decisions was leaving my job, asking my partner to leave hers and starting a company with financial liabilities and a baby on the way. I've always believed that working from home doesn't work as effectively in India. My HR team often urges me to reconsider, but I stand by my belief that the work culture we've developed requires in-person collaboration. Maybe future generations, who have experienced schooling from home, will adapt better to remote work, but for us, the physical office is essential. Taking these steps has been risky, but they've shaped who I am as a leader and how we've built this company.

Data and Digital Have Driven the Growth of Public Relations

The initial days of PR centred on fundamentals: press releases, media kits and building relationships with traditional media sources. The goal was simple—shaping public perception by getting the appropriate message out.

However, PR has come a long way. Press release distribution and relationship-building have evolved. Today, PR is integrated with digital marketing, social media, data analytics and even artificial intelligence. But how?

The digital revolution: The internet flipped the script. Its advent in the 1990s was the turning point in the development of PR. Brands eventually could communicate directly with their audiences through press releases, email newsletters and websites. However, with social media emerging in the 2000s, there was another shift. PR professionals now had direct channels of connection with target audiences through platforms like Facebook, Instagram, LinkedIn and X, creating direct engagement opportunities.

Brands can now create communities, have real-time conversations and quickly respond to crises, turning PR from an ineffective one-way street into an active two-way dialogue.

The age of data: Over the past decade, data has become an essential element of PR success measurement. Traditional methods like media clippings and impressions have been replaced by more sophisticated metrics, such as sentiment analysis tools and social listening platforms, which allow PR professionals to monitor brand mentions and determine ROI more rapidly than ever.

PR today is driven by data. Social media analytics, sentiment analysis tools, and web traffic tools have allowed brands to understand their audiences better and make more informed decisions.

The changing face of PR: Modern PR can best be described as integrated, multichannel and highly focused on authenticity. It includes telling captivating stories across platforms such as social media, content marketing and influencer partnerships. PR professionals now work alongside marketing and advertising teams to craft campaigns that connect more closely with audiences on an emotional level.

The key takeaway for PR professionals: adapt, innovate, practice and always stay ahead of the curve.

19

Valerie Pinto

CEO, Weber Shandwick India

'My entry into public relations was both unexpected and fascinating.'

Inspired by My Aunt to Make a Career in Public Relations

I was born and raised in Mumbai. I lost my father when I was just two years old, and my mother single-handedly raised my sister and me. From a young age, I learnt the values of collaboration and discipline. While other children were playing outdoors, I often helped my mother and sister with household chores. I developed a passion for sports and dreamed of pursuing it seriously, but circumstances led me to focus on my education instead. This dedication paid off when I graduated as the top student in economics. I studied economics and political science at St Xavier's College, Mumbai.

I had to start working early in life, and my entry into public relations was both unexpected and fascinating. While working at the Taj Mahal Palace Hotel in Mumbai, I was introduced to marketing communications through tasks like writing brochures, which sparked my interest in the field. Another significant influence was my aunt, who served as the head of corporate communications at L&T for many years. Her success and career path left a lasting impression on me, inspiring me to pursue a similar direction and eventually leading me to a fulfilling career in public relations.

My career began early, with my first significant role as a corporate communications manager at UTV. The position came with a substantial salary for someone at that stage of life. However, a pivotal moment came when the CFO of UTV advised me to pursue a professional degree and gain broader exposure by working with multiple brands in consultancies before transitioning back to corporate roles. He believed this approach would enable me to add greater value to any organisation in the future. So, after a course in communications at the Xavier's Institute of Communications, I joined Perfect Relations and started with a modest salary of ₹3,000. This role proved transformative, as managing investor relations accounts exposed me to a diverse range of clients and helped me build a strong foundation in public relations. Living in Mumbai, the financial capital of India, I naturally developed an affinity for the banking sector. Global companies like American Express, MasterCard and Goldman Sachs became my clients later. My dedication and results-driven approach led to rapid growth—I was appointed COO of Perfect Relations at the age of twenty-five and ascended to the position of CEO by twenty-eight.

I dedicated approximately sixteen years to Perfect Relations, gaining invaluable experience and expertise in the field. For the past ten years, I have been with Weber Shandwick, continuing to grow and evolve in my career.

I have a passion for cooking and baking, and I find immense joy in preparing meals and sharing them with others. During the pandemic, that's exactly how I spent my time—creating and serving dishes for my friends, neighbours and family.

20

Xavier Prabhu

Founder, PR Hub

'The universe has a plan for each of us, like a jigsaw puzzle. We don't need to know the entire plan upfront; instead, we should focus on solving each piece as it comes.'

The Aspiring Scientist Who Moved to Public Relations

I was born in 1971 near Salem, Tamil Nadu, in a district now called Krishnagiri. My mom was a homemaker, and my dad had moved there for his teaching job. Being a school teacher, my dad likely had no exposure to the world of business, marketing, branding or communication. The focus in our family was always on traditional careers—engineering, medicine, law and civil services.

I went to primary school in Krishnagiri. I studied at St James Higher Secondary School near Trichy until the tenth grade in Tamil medium. For grades eleven and twelve, I switched to English and went to Don Bosco School in Tirupathur. Like most students, I was probably just considering a career in engineering since I didn't have any interest in medicine.

My talent as a speaker laid the foundation for what came later. I was a good orator and won numerous debating and elocution competitions in school. I was also good at writing, winning several essay competitions.

While my brothers pursued engineering, I enrolled at the Government Arts College in Krishnagiri for my undergraduate studies. I wasn't particularly interested in academics. I was more involved in extracurricular activities. I was the debating society secretary, class representative, hostel captain and took on other leadership roles.

After graduation, I decided to join Loyola College in Chennai to pursue my master's degree in physics. This was a tough period in my life. I was studying for something I wasn't truly invested in, yet I couldn't quite figure out what path I should be on. After completing my postgraduation studies, the expectation was to start working. But research was also an option with a master's degree.

I started exploring opportunities for further research, applying to top institutions like the Tata Institute of Fundamental Research and the Institute of Astrophysics in Pune. Eventually, I was selected by the Physical Research Laboratory in Ahmedabad. The programme would have led to a doctorate and potentially opened doors to joining ISRO or a similar organisation as a scientist. However, even with these prestigious options, I was struggling to align my interests with what I was doing.

Despite following this path, which seemed like the natural progression for someone in my position—especially after having published research on high-temperature superconductors in collaboration with Anna University and

IIT Madras—I made a sudden decision to not pursue it. This choice surprised and disappointed my parents. Turning away from such a secure, respectable career was a risky move for someone belonging to a middle-class family where stability was highly valued.

One of my acquaintances from Loyola College had an uncle who owned an advertising agency called Corp Media Men (CMM) Advertising in Chennai. I went to his office, and they gave me a copywriting test. The next morning, I received a call saying that my writing showed promise and that I seemed to have a creative flair. They offered me a position as a trainee copywriter.

That's how my career in the world of advertising and communications began. At that point, I still had no idea about PR. I just knew that I wanted to do something far removed from science or engineering. I craved a creative outlet, and this opportunity felt like the right fit.

I stayed with the agency for a while, and they groomed me for growth. Soon I was promoted to junior copywriter. Due to high cost of living in Chennai, I needed to keep my options open, so when I saw that National Advertising, one of the top ten agencies in India at the time, had an opening for a copywriter in their Bangalore office, I applied and got selected for the job. The offer came with a salary that was more than double of what I was earning.

I moved to Bangalore and joined National Advertising. During this period, in 1994, I came across an article about the growing field of public relations in India, which was starting to gain importance as a result of liberalisation.

The article mentioned a PR firm called Melcole PR, which was an affiliate of Ketchum in India. Intrigued by the prospect of a new career direction, I decided to reach out to them. Even though my experience at National Advertising was fulfilling, I felt that the growth trajectory there would be slow and steady, and I was eager to explore new opportunities.

I took a chance by reaching out to Melcole PR, and it turned out to be a stroke of luck. The next morning, I received a call back saying that Mr M.L. Kaul and Ms Praveen Ricky, who were running Melcole, happened to be in Bangalore.

It felt like an incredible coincidence—reading the article, and then the MDs being in town just as I reached out. It seemed like destiny. I met with them, and shortly afterward, they asked me to join Melcole PR's Bangalore branch as a manager.

This was how I began my career in PR. The timing was almost serendipitous: I hadn't known much about PR until I read that article, and within a week of discovering it, I had an offer from a PR firm. I started at Melcole a month later and discovered my true passion for the field.

Melcole was a smaller firm with limited growth opportunities due to its hierarchical structure. As someone eager to advance and learn more, I sought new challenges. That's when Corporate Voice Weber Shandwick, a much larger and globally recognised firm, offered me a position as an associate consultant.

Joining Corporate Voice Weber Shandwick was a significant cultural shock for me. Having come from a smaller town and transitioned to Bangalore, I was exposed to a very different environment there. The firm attracted top talent from elite sections of metropolitan areas, and I found myself in a world where appearance, personal branding and understanding complex social dynamics were crucial.

Until then, I had been relatively sheltered, focusing on my skills and performance rather than how I presented myself. I quickly learnt that packaging oneself effectively and navigating the corporate culture were just as important as the work itself. It took about a year or more to adapt to these new expectations. This experience taught me a valuable lesson about the importance of presenting yourself and navigating corporate dynamics.

Around this time India was also experiencing a surge in entrepreneurship and start-ups, which added another exciting layer to the landscape. Wanting to make the most of such opportunities, I launched PR Hub, a portal designed to serve as both a knowledge base and a connecting point for the PR firms. While the venture was quite innovative it didn't get the recognition it might have deserved, partly because I didn't publicise it extensively. If I had the clarity I have now, things might have been different, but I don't regret the journey. Life unfolds as it does, and you adapt and move forward.

Soon after, Symbiosis reached out to me, asking if I could help shape their curriculum on online PR and also teach their students. The director believed that since I had started PR Hub, I must be an expert in online PR, which was anticipated to become a major field. He invited me to speak to an entire batch. It was a surreal day. A former physics master's student specialising in solid-state physics who had shifted from a potential career in science to becoming a copywriter and then an entrepreneur discussing online PR. I was both amused and astonished by the turn my career had taken.

I continued exploring various avenues. One notable endeavour was attempting to develop a platform similar to PR Newswire and Business Wire. We aimed to create a service where users could find PR partners and clients. However, within a year or so, it became clear that this approach wasn't financially viable.

One significant hindrance was that many journalists in India were using outdated systems with limited, text-based functionalities. This lack of modern infrastructure meant that any new product we developed wouldn't have had a market. The obstacles we faced underscored the difficulties in trying to introduce new technology in an environment that wasn't ready for it.

It's fundamental now to conduct market research before developing a product, but at the time I was an entrepreneur eager to dive in. We faced a problem with product development. We initially wanted to create a platform where consultancies could find support in different cities. For instance, even if a Delhi-based firm needed coverage in Bangalore, they found it hard to pay for a listing on PR Hub. They preferred to use their own connections instead, which highlighted a critical flaw in our revenue model. Second, we had anticipated that revenue from these services would fund product development, but the plan quickly became unviable. The investors, though supportive, felt that the market wasn't ready for our vision and preferred to not wait for it to mature. I could either continue personally funding the venture or shut it down.

Around this time, I spoke to a former colleague who had become the editor of a major technology magazine in India. He advised me to retain the PR Hub brand, as it had value and potential. He suggested I pivot rather than pursue a failing venture, noting that the hype around start-ups was overstated and not worth chasing.

His advice was crucial. It prevented me from sinking further into a failing idea and helped me focus on leveraging the PR Hub brand in a more sustainable way.

One of the turning points came when a former client from my time at the previous job reached out. He said, 'Xavier, I always thought you were great to work with. How about doing PR for us in India?' At the time, I was deeply immersed in my PR Hub, but his offer made me reconsider. He gave me a piece of advice that has stuck with me: 'Business is about making money. If you're not making money, you're not really in business. At least with me, you'll have a steady income.'

I also received another offer from East West PR, a firm in Singapore. They were looking for support for a major roadshow and were willing to pay good money. With these two offers on the table, it became difficult to believe that my online PR project was taking off as expected. It was time for PR Hub to become a boutique PR firm.

I rented a small office in central Bangalore and hired a few people. My first employee was Pooja Iyer and my first client was Force Computers. I soon began receiving more work from PR firms in Mumbai and Delhi.

With clients and revenue coming in steadily, the firm grew rapidly. We quickly moved to a larger office to accommodate our expanding team. While I hadn't initially planned to focus solely on traditional PR, the business's growth and the consistent income it provided made it clear that this was the direction to follow.

We faced two main challenges initially. First, the clients we were working with through other consultancies weren't willing to pay as much as direct clients would, and second, we were missing out on the branding and direct experience that comes from working with clients. So, we decided to focus solely on acquiring and managing direct clients.

This shift laid the groundwork for PR Hub's evolution. Within a year, we opened our office in Chennai. By the third year, we had established a presence in Delhi, and by the fifth or sixth year, we expanded to Mumbai. Between 2008 and 2011, we had a national footprint.

This period showed me that focusing on direct client relationships and expanding our firm was the right path. We were also among the early adopters of investing in design and digital capabilities. We even attempted to create a creative boutique within PR Hub, under the brand MindSparks, and a separate digital entity, PR Hub Digital. While these ventures didn't take off as we had hoped, they provided valuable lessons. The experience deepened our expertise in creative and digital domains.

Sumathi Chari, a co-partner, played a crucial role in our journey. She shared my passion for communication and creativity. Her enthusiasm mirrored mine, making her a valuable partner over the past two decades.

One memorable campaign I led was with a major industrial gases company, where I developed a safety training programme with the Institute of Welding. Initially, there was little interest, but after a year and a half of hard work, the programme became integral to their business and continues to generate value. This success highlighted the power of communication in creating lasting programs that align with business needs.

I have pushed boundaries throughout my career. For instance, at Melcole, we worked with UB Networks, a company competing against giants like Cisco in the Ethernet router and hub market. Instead of trying to compete directly with their resources, I focused on creative strategies. I conducted in-depth research and went beyond traditional media relations to find innovative ways to position UB Networks effectively.

I met directly with the country head and marketing head and told them that raising awareness was crucial for breaking through the competitive landscape. Simply trying to get media coverage wouldn't suffice against major players like Cisco. The country head appreciated my approach so much that they wrote a letter thanking me for going beyond my duties. As a result, we developed a networking booklet—a straightforward, collaborative effort that my firm initially dismissed as irrelevant. The booklet turned out to be a significant success, and the founder of the company went on to establish one of India's largest start-ups.

In another instance, we pitched to a medical subscription company. I predicted that technology would disrupt their business model and suggested they reposition themselves accordingly. The MD was sceptical and questioned whether a PR firm should be discussing business strategy. They decided to exclude me from the pitch. A few years later, I saw a news article about the company pivoting their business model precisely as I had predicted. It was a confidence booster, affirming that my strategic insights were on point.

My story reflects a deep commitment to following my heart. I often share a philosophy I believe in: the universe has a plan for each of us, like a jigsaw puzzle. We don't need to know the entire plan upfront; instead, we should focus on solving each piece as it comes. This belief allows me to embrace risks with confidence, knowing that each step is part of a greater design.

21

Sharif Rangnekar

Former CEO, Integral PR

'My diverse experiences—shaped by a family that celebrated intellectualism, artistry and resilience—have profoundly influenced who I am today.'

A Gradual Transition from Journalism to Public Relations

I was born in Mumbai to a family that deeply valued music, art, nature and food. My upbringing was infused with creativity and intellectual curiosity.

My father was a renowned economist and editor of *The Economic Times*. He was also recognised as a futurologist and was one of two Indians featured in *Time* magazine's 1977 list of the 350 leaders shaping the world. It was a remarkable achievement, especially considering India's global standing at the time. My father held a doctorate in economics and was among the few of his generation to graduate from the prestigious London School of Economics.

My mother, a Bharatanatyam dancer, was equally remarkable. Her creativity extended to designing and tailoring her own clothes, some of which were showcased in a leading women's magazine of the 1970s. She was also an early enthusiast of bonsai art and later became a naturopath after my father's passing, blending traditional healing methods with her artistic sensibilities. Her innovative use of Natya Shastra as part of her healing practice was far ahead of its time.

Growing up, music was a constant presence in our lives. From classical concerts to family outings at Hanging Gardens near Malabar Hill, our home was filled with lively discussions and creative influences. I attended Bombay International School in Babulnath, and those formative years laid the foundation for my eclectic interests.

When my father left *The Economic Times* to become the editor of *Business Standard*, we moved to Calcutta. We lived in New Alipore while his office was in Central Calcutta, part of the iconic ABP Group office just off Chowringhee. After his untimely passing in 1984, our family moved to Delhi, where he had built a home intended for his retirement. I completed my schooling at Frank Anthony Public School.

My career began in publishing shortly after college, a choice driven more by necessity than passion. Ironically, I disliked it, despite my later success as an author and organiser of a literary festival. I soon transitioned to journalism, influenced by family expectations. Despite being introverted, I gradually found joy in the field, working with notable mentors like Vinod Mehta and Paranjoy Guha Thakurta at *The Pioneer*, and later joining *The Economic Times*. I started in the corporate bureau before moving to the economic bureau under M.K. Venu, whose mentorship left a lasting impact on me.

In 2000, I left mainstream media with Venu to join e-indiabiznews.com, which was gaining momentum. I collaborated on a news and research initiative, supplying content to platforms like *Tehelka* and newspapertoday.com (part of the then India Today Group). However, the dot-com bust of 2001 was a harsh reality check.

The foray into web-based news was my first experience with the emerging digital media landscape. However, the initiative was short-lived and eventually became part of a larger group of companies engaged in public relations, public affairs and related fields.

During this transition, I began exploring content enhancement for PR, incorporating elements of public affairs. Simultaneously, we attempted to market content, but neither Venu nor I felt entirely suited to this role. Venu chose to return to *The Economic Times*, while I decided to stay back, initially managing the content division and later serving as a director on the board of Integral PR.

When the CEO of Integral PR resigned, I was hesitant to step into the role. I wasn't convinced that PR was my true calling, nor did I have experience running a business. For a brief period, the position was filled by Kunal Sachdev, a well-known marketing professional, but when he moved to Bangalore, the opportunity came to me again. This time, I decided to give it a shot, provided I had the autonomy to run the company my way and select my own chairman.

That decision marked the beginning of my active involvement in PR, a journey that lasted over a decade. During this time, I also became involved with PRCAI, eventually serving as its president. I played a role in reforming the association's governance with a set of other leaders, introducing a more democratic election process and amending its constitution to better serve the profession's evolving needs.

One of my significant contributions was bringing the SABRE Awards to India in collaboration with fellow leaders like Nikhil Dey, Arun Sudhaman and Paul Holmes. While SABRE had never done a country-specific award before, we worked to create a South Asia edition. This initiative, along with the return of the ICCO Summit to India, reflected the growing prominence of the PR profession in the region.

These years were transformative for the profession, which was beginning to assert its importance within the broader communication landscape. My early years in PR were fuelled by a journalist's curiosity—a desire to learn and explore. However, my professional journey was also deeply intertwined with my personal one, particularly my experiences as a gay man navigating societal expectations and work challenges.

In my early years, I faced fear and was cautious. Friends in the corporate and PR worlds warned me that coming out could harm my career in a largely conservative corporate world. Concerns about reputation and societal judgment often dictated business relationships. However, over time, I witnessed encouraging signs of open-mindedness within the communications fraternity.

While much progress has been made, there's still a long way to go in fostering inclusivity. My personal journey towards self-expression and freedom became a critical part of my professional narrative. Coming out is inherently political—it challenges societal norms, fights systemic biases and often involves confronting legislators, governments and even media stereotypes.

These experiences inspired me to push back against the rigid boxes that marketing and PR often reinforce—be it gender roles, aspirations or societal expectations. To 'queer' narratives is to challenge and expand them, reflecting the diversity and fluidity of modern identities. Today's younger audiences are deeply invested in their chosen identities and resist being confined by labels, prompting a shift in how we communicate and engage with consumers.

Ultimately, my thirty-year journey across journalism and PR has been about learning, unlearning and applying my skills to both professional and personal pursuits. Stepping away from conventional roles allowed me to embrace my individuality while leveraging the tools and insights I've gained to contribute to meaningful change in the profession and beyond.

Over the years, I've explored various creative avenues alongside my career in PR. For instance, I began delving into music and poetry. In 2013, I wrote and performed a song at the Hard Rock Café, marking my debut as a somewhat disorganised singer-songwriter.

That performance turned out to be India's first musical dedication to the LGBTQIA+ community. It was especially poignant because it coincided with the Supreme Court's decision to decriminalise homosexuality. Writing and performing were extensions of my passion for communication—finding unique ways to engage, share ideas and advocate for change. It aligned with what we often do in PR: using storytelling to inspire thought and action.

This creative journey became an exploration of communication and freedom, blending my personal and professional aspirations. I managed Integral PR for about eleven years, starting as a director in 2003 before stepping into the role of CEO.

During my tenure, the firm grew and evolved. When I initially joined, the PR profession itself was relatively small. Early on, one of our significant achievements was securing KPMG as a client. At the time, they weren't as prominent in the 'Big Four' landscape and were an ideal fit for my journalistic background. KPMG's focus on thought leadership and research, rather than just selling services, allowed us to position them as a leader over four to six years.

This account also marked a pivotal shift for the consultancy, as KPMG measured our output against outcomes—something rare in the profession at the time. Their partners' KRAs became the benchmark for our work, pushing us to engage directly with leadership and present at partner offsites. This elevated the consultancy's role, allowing us to demonstrate the strategic value of PR at the boardroom level.

Another significant early win was Audi. Working directly with Audi's global teams in Germany, we went beyond execution to contribute ideas and strategy. For example, we coordinated high-profile photo shoots at iconic locations like India Gate and the Taj Mahal, navigating government approvals to make these campaigns possible. Audi's global reports, which resembled luxurious coffee table books, required us to identify and help bring on influential figures like Vir Sanghvi to position the brand as more than just an automobile company—it became a symbol of an aspirational lifestyle.

In the realm of crisis management, we worked on numerous accounts, but the lack of proper measurement in the PR profession has always been a point of contention for me. Unlike advertising, where metrics are well-defined, the impact of repairing or protecting reputations in crises often goes unquantified. This disparity is a disservice we do to ourselves as a profession.

One campaign that stands out from my time working with Reckitt (then RB) was centred around building Dettol's position in the hygiene space. The campaign leveraged the Global Hygiene Council and was entirely content-driven. Unlike traditional product promotions, we didn't push press releases about new products or fragrances. Instead, we focused on creating awareness around hygiene through data, research and stakeholder engagement.

This content-led strategy helped Dettol outperform its competitors, including Lifebuoy, which was running controversial campaigns at the time. We worked with medical and other experts to amplify messages about hygiene and personal care, achieving results that rivalled advertising campaigns. This initiative eventually laid the foundation for the Dettol Surakshit Parivar programme, which evolved into the now-renowned Banega Swachh India campaign in partnership with NDTV. The campaign earned a Diamond SABRE Award.

Another memorable campaign involved a now-defunct start-up called Growth Enabler, which helped other start-ups secure funding. Despite being a small account with a modest fee, it was a strategic entry into this ecosystem for us. Our efforts included creating multi-stakeholder strategies, hosting events, leveraging data and research and securing speaking opportunities for the founders. These efforts directly contributed to the start-up's first round of funding, showcasing the tangible business outcomes PR can deliver. Growth Enabler's unique positioning as a platform for start-ups made this campaign particularly rewarding.

These successes marked a transformative period for Integral PR. We moved from typical consumer media relations to more sophisticated accounts, requiring significant changes in staffing and operations. Early on, there was considerable churn as we built teams capable of handling these high-profile accounts.

The Rainbow Literary Festival is another project close to my heart. Starting in 2019, we faced the challenge of carving out space for queer literature in a market dominated by mainstream literary festivals. At that time, there was minimal recognition of LGBTQIA+ literature as a distinct genre.

Given my background in journalism and PR, and with just one book to my name, I didn't have a natural foothold in the literary world. To address this, we collaborated with AvianWE to form an advisory committee comprising established authors, journalists, consultants on inclusion and human rights advocates. While we needed their guidance and input, their presence gave the festival credibility and allowed us to meaningfully engage publishers, media and audiences.

The festival's impact was recognised through several awards, including the SABRE Certificate of Excellence, Fulcrum Awards and ET Brand Equity honours. Internally, the team working on this account won an ACE Award for our collaborative work.

Across all these campaigns, the common thread has been a focus on driving meaningful outcomes—whether in reputation, funding or societal change. These experiences underscore the transformative power of strategic PR.

My diverse experiences—shaped by a family that celebrated intellectualism, artistry and resilience—have profoundly influenced who I am today. Each phase of my life has been a testament to the unpredictable yet enriching journey of self-discovery. These experiences represent a blend of creativity, strategy and advocacy—values that have shaped both my professional and personal journey.

From Being Irrelevant to Becoming Essential

The PR profession two decades ago had hardly any stature, which isn't the case today. When I took up the role as the CEO of a PR firm in November 2004, the profession was highly discredited, particularly by the press. Even corporations saw most consultancies as execution arms, implying that the PR fraternity lacked sufficient depth and intellect, and therefore wasn't seen as a value-driven practice that could play a strategic role in their larger communications plans.

It was a fact, though, that most of the business on offer then was limited to press releases and briefings, launches and ribbon cutting events and daily news reports. The efforts revolved around getting clients column centimetres of coverage in the media. That reality had left PR itself being viewed as media relations, an unfortunate synonymity that came in the way of a positive change in perception or growth in retainer fees. And low margins due to those circumstances meant only a handful of players could invest in knowledge and content.

Still, this change was bound to come. It was in the simple steps of investing in information and studied inspection of the content collated that showed we knew how to make sense of news. It was a shift from counting clips and calculating ad value (a horribly flawed comparison between editorial content and bought space) to assessing whether the news was positive, impactful in terms of brand value and perception. Around then, the efforts were about aligning communications strategies with business objectives of an organisation and, therefore, measurable returns on investment.

In a sense, the profession started to shift its role from output to outcome, from the periphery to a meaningful partner of strategic value. In multiple ways, we were moving away from reliance on the media to gradually emerge as an important outreach arm for corporations' plans. We were being seen as communicators, often sitting at the same table as admen and lawyers, getting closer and closer to the boardroom.

Undoubtedly, the rise of social media and digital platforms led us to become more involved in data and how to use the same to develop messages, identify audiences and even prepare for crisis situations. How the business built talent pools was changing as hiring from the worlds of finance and banking, hospitality, healthcare, advertising and real estate took place.

While we continue to be compared with advertising and its system of measurement amidst insufficient discussion on the role of PR in the area of crisis, the greatest acknowledgement of the profession came during the election campaign of 2014.

Although this was a turning point in India's political history, it was a period where politicians and their coteries of advisors realised the value of thought out, strategic communications, picking up from practices that corporations had adopted over the years. As a consequence, the PM candidate had a messaging strategy in place with localised narratives depending on the audience or the region, and listening tools as well, to amend a strategy or build on one. It also underlined the arrival of something that PR folks were creating, which is an integral part of most campaigns, a 360-degree outreach plan that uses multiple tools and media to reach and captivate diverse audiences, addressing demographics, location, languages, economics, emotions and more.

Since then, the growth has been exponential as the profession itself has shown its ability to connect with the changing ideas, aspirations and pride of Indians at large. In a sense, PR now has a far better connect with the politics of our nation, therefore, it is closer to the pulse of the people. Which is why, much like ad firms and media that look for government advertising, even PR firms are being called in more and more by governments and state-owned enterprises to handle their image.

Over these two decades, the journey covered and the evolution made is remarkable, where PR went from being somewhat irrelevant to a function that cannot be ignored.

22

Rekha Rao

Founder and CEO, OON

'I have gone beyond the conventional to drive genuine, long-lasting impact.'

From a Simple Life to the World of Big Brands in Mumbai

As a child of the 1970s, I grew up in a typical middle-class Indian family. We had limited exposure and access to the world, without the internet and mobile phones, making life much simpler, with fewer distractions.

At barely the age of eleven I used to keep a scrapbook of ads that I liked, cut from Sunday's glossy supplements and magazines brought home by Dad. I was fascinated and intrigued by the snappy headlines, bright colours and pretty pictures. While no one at home knew about advertising as a profession, I was convinced that this was what I wanted to do.

I was my 'academically inclined' mother's worst nightmare. My two older sisters were conscientious about their studies while I played truant. When I scored 83% in my main subjects in my 10th boards, my mother was in utter disbelief. She thought I could be her doctor or engineer daughter. But I chose to study commerce, as it had the thinnest textbooks. To my mom's surprise, I got admission into the only college in Hyderabad that offered B. Com (Hons.), after ranking fourth in the competitive entrance exam, and she started hoping that I may become a chartered accountant.

But I was set on writing ads. Unfortunately, Osmania University did not offer advertising as a subject. I asked Mom if I could go to Bombay for my further studies only to get a ferocious scowl and an earful about 'I could go wherever after I got married'. Fortunately, fate intervened. My sister who married someone from Indore figured that Devi Ahilya University offered a post-graduate diploma in advertising and public relations. After reassurances from my sister and brother-in-law that I would be under strict supervision, my mom let me go. I went on to win a Gold Medal, making my mom proud, and thaw a little towards advertising.

My first job was as a trainee copywriter with Rahul Jain's Swift Advertising (later acquired by Percept) in Indore. I got access to some of the best advertising books and my first computer here. Eighteen months later I got an offer from Uxhur. A 50 per cent increment and the opportunity to work in a Bombay-based agency made me leave Rahul bhai's agency. In less than a year, this agency ran into trouble due to massive financial mismanagement, leaving me scared and without a salary for months.

An advertising veteran was appointed to clean up the mess. He started by shutting down unprofitable branches while keeping the promising ones running. When he arrived in Indore, I didn't know if I would have a job by the time he left. This CEO was Jameel Gulrays. He saw the eagerness and genuine effort of the team (Ashish, Mridul, Juhi, and I) and signed off on keeping the branch running. I was elevated to the post of the branch head. Just twenty-two years old and petrified, I refused to take this up, but Jameel egged me on by simply saying, 'You'll learn. I'll guide you.'

Soon our work relationship transformed into a soul connection. At work, I was in awe of him, overwhelmed by his knowledge and celebrity status in advertising. At a personal level, Jameel's brutal honesty had me starry-eyed, as I had never met anyone so fearless with truth.

But to a very young and naïve me, this choice was a hard battle. Our relationship defied every conventional, Indian societal norm—age, religion, culture, marital status, work dynamics—everything incendiary that could burn us both at multiple levels. Yet, I chose him.

What followed is a story for a five-season OTT series. But finally, in January 1997, I was in Bombay, the city of my dreams, the mecca of advertising. After forty-five days of a frantic job search, I landed one with Chaitra Leo Burnett as a copywriter, on P&G's Ariel. I quit after a short stint, to move to Ammirati Puris Lintas (now Lowe), as a bilingual (English and Hindi) writer on Unilever's Clinic Plus, Clinic All Clear, and later Nihar. After two years of writing hair commercials, I moved to Triton where I was writing copy for everything from a vacuum cleaner, to engine oil, to cooking oil, to chai and more.

When Jameel's MSME clients started requesting end-to-end execution in addition to advertising strategy, we set up Versatile Communications to provide print, film, radio production; events; media buying—everything communications. However, in November 2003, my mom was diagnosed with cancer. My second sister and I were primary caregivers, as she underwent treatment, first in Pune, then in Mumbai's Tata Cancer Hospital. The still-new Versatile Communications took a back seat, affecting business. Mom passed away in February 2005. With my finances at an all-time low, I was adamant about returning to the safety of a job and a regular salary, even as Jameel wanted us to re-energise Versatile.

I applied for jobs in both advertising and PR firms. The quickest response came from PR consultancies, with my first interview at IPAN (now Burson). The meeting with Radhika Shapoorjee went like a breeze. At the age of thirty-five, I marked my entry into the world of PR.

Baptism by fire would be an understatement about my introduction to PR. Monsanto, Lifebuoy, Fair and Lovely, and CRY were my clients. On day one at work, I got a call a couple of hours into the job with a client asking me to send, him an updated media list. My senior-most team member said, 'Chill boss, I'll send it.' Within 30 minutes I got a call from a now furious client, yelling about how we sent him an outdated list. I was convinced this thing called media list was a troublemaker!

Nothing we did as far as the said client went was right. Things weren't any better with the other clients. I seemed to be constantly in the GM's room, seeking help. By the end of month three, I broke down and told my boss I didn't know how to cope. He shrugged and said, 'If you can't handle it, quit.'

The next working day, I told my team we would never again walk into the GM's room asking for help. My copy and advertising background helped me look at PR beyond media relations, and we went on to create some of the biggest campaigns, many firsts, and stellar work that set an example in Unilever and the consultancy. And I never did seek help from my boss again. This happened because I decided to take complete charge of my team and clients to move ahead.

When I moved to Corporate Voice Weber Shandwick in February 2012, my primary task was to help retain and grow the P&G mandate. Thanks to Atul Ahluwalia, I learnt the art of writing award entries here. My work on P&G's Gillette and Vicks alongside campaigns Thank You Mom and Project Shiksha, picked up my first haul of seven SABRE Awards. There was no looking back.

I then joined 2020 MSL, Mumbai, as general manager in September 2013. The challenge of building a consumer practice in a B2B tech consultancy was just what I needed.

Glenn Osaki, the then president of MSL APAC, called me one day in early April 2017 and said, 'Rekha, you have created what very few professionals ever get an opportunity to create, or can only dream of creating.' This was the week after the Vicks Touch of Care campaign went viral, and became a global conversation in advertising and PR circles. This film featured Gauri Sawant, a transgender activist.

After we won the pitch for Vicks in September 2016, the campaign was to go live in the next quarter. However, demonetisation derailed the launch, and the beautiful film got canned. In March 2017, Prachi Partagalkar from Publicis Singapore called and said, 'Rekha, we've created a beautiful film, and we think this is worthy of Cannes. But with no budgets, all the big plans have been shelved. Is it possible for you to help us with some support, just a press release to A&M media, so we can at least back the entry with some coverage?' I asked her to send me the film, to explore what could be done. One look at the film and intuitively I knew we could do something big with it. While my business sense said, no money, no time, the creative devil in me just could not let this go.

We devised a strategy to not just reach out to the A&M media, but also pitch the story to general news channels and publications. The team frowned and said, 'But they just want A&M!' But they knew me well enough not to argue, so Shubhangi Chaturvedi and Amala Hosagrahar went about doing what was asked.

This was the year the Supreme Court case for decriminalisation of Article 377 was nearing its close. If we went ahead with the plan to talk to consumer media, the first task was to get Gauri Sawant to trust us enough to agree to be the media face of the campaign. The risk: she was not a trained spokesperson. She could be high-strung and emotional. And as a transgender activist, she could be easily drawn into a conversation on Article 377, completely derailing the messaging and the intent of our campaign.

I spent a full day at her home, in the slums of Malad (a suburb of Mumbai), sitting on her cot, chatting with her and her *chelaas* (followers), eating and drinking with them. At the end of the day, she hugged me and said she would work with me.

With Gauri on board, we took Publicis' Ajay Trivikraman and Prachi Partagalkar into confidence. We took Ritu Mittal, the marketing lead for Vicks in India, through our plan, covering bases for the brand in a politically, ideologically, religiously, and socially divided India. Every negative scenario and the brand's response was thrashed out. A strong backstory was put in place, focusing on 'where there is care, there is family'. Gauri passionately expounded our message 'motherhood knows no gender'.

We had a narrative that captured the mind, and a film that stole hearts. Within twenty-four hours of our well-planned interviews, our phone started ringing non-stop for a story with Gauri. Four days later, a very excited Prachi called me and said, 'Congratulations, Rekha. You guys did it. The Vicks film has gone viral.' I thought I misheard the 'you guys did it' part. So Prachi repeated, 'No. I mean PR has made the campaign viral. We could not activate YouTube due to some glitch. We are just seventy-two hours into the campaign and already have four million views.' As it hit me, I screamed out to my team, 'Guys, Vicks has gone viral because of PR.' We drove stories with top global media—NPR, CNN, the ad being played at the UN-New York Times Women in the World Summit in front of world leaders like Justin Trudeau and Hillary Clinton. Gauri featuring on the show *Kaun Banega Crorepati* and more such opportunities ensured that Vicks swept every award that year.

By the time I left, 2020 MSL was a strong consumer and brand PR firm, along with being a B2B tech specialist. My proudest moment was when 2020 MSL was listed in Campaign Brief Asia's 2020 Asia Creative Rankings as one of the hottest creative consultancies in Asia alongside advertising and creative agencies, and as one of the top twenty of India's hottest firms. My greatest gratification is also when marketing leaders redirect budgets to PR, recognising its superior returns.

My next move as the managing director of Zeno India happened just before the global COVID-19 shutdown. As I navigated the highs and lows of the pandemic and post-pandemic years, I set up a robust technology practice, with my trusted partner and friend Ketan Pote joining me from 2020 MSL. While I enjoyed my job, I missed active consumer brand work, and campaign creation work for corporates and brands. So, I inched out of Zeno, to create my next big—Oon, a British dialectal for 'one'. This is arguably the world's first women's collective providing integrated marketing solutions.

If there is ever an epitaph written for me, I would like it to read: 'Here lies a woman who defined her life with unconventional choices and worked passionately to prove these were the best.'

23

Amitabh Saksena

Founder and Managing Director, Actimedia PR & Digital

'Don't run after money, let the money pursue you. You go on doing what you truly love and enjoy.'

From Sales to the Universe of Lifestyle Public Relations

Growing up, I was always in awe of how my parents skilfully managed their responsibilities while still engaging in social work and community activities. Their multitasking abilities combined with my college project on 'Trusteeship' at St Xavier's College, Mumbai, and insights from E.F. Schumacher's *Small is Beautiful*, laid the foundation for Actimedia. Today, Actimedia stands as a boutique firm specialising in lifestyle advisory, driven by our motto: 'Happy People Happy Clients'.

I was born in Nagpur and grew up reading voraciously. The likes of Enid Blyton and Milind Kundera were my great companions. My father worked for the Indian Railways and for some time he was deputed to theWestern Coalfields, which made my childhood magical. Travelling to places like Nagpur, Bilaspur, Jabalpur and Mumbai gave me a good understanding of geographies, people and economies. Getting to see coal mines, steel and aluminium plants, paper mills, cloth mills and hydel power plants was a world of sheer enchantment.

I graduated from St Xavier's College and pursued a master's degree in economics from the University of Mumbai, followed by an MBA.

I secured an internship at ACC Cements during my business programme, but quickly realised sales wasn't my forte. In my second year I came across an article in *Business Today* on PR and how it was the sunrise profession—and the rest is history. I applied to the three firms mentioned in the article and I was fortunate that one of them, Ravi Shyam & Associates, hired me. Ravi, a PR veteran, helped lay a solid foundation for my career. From day one, he involved me in strategising, client meetings and, of course, I got my hands dirty with scanning newspapers, cutting and pasting clips and faxing them. It was quite a journey working with brands like Lee Jeans, France Telecom and Al Futtaim Watches, among others. I was soon picked up by IPAN (a Hill & Knowlton Associate), where I worked with some of the best brands in the world—Goldman Sachs, PWC, Nokia, MTV, Cisco, and HCL.

It was at IPAN that I met my business partner, Binita Bodani Putcha, who actually goaded me to start Actimedia. Our journey began with Esso Petroleum, who wanted PR assistance for the Esso Awards for Tiger Conservation. We never looked back after that.

Today, Actimedia has two other allied verticals—influencer marketing and Actimedia Earth—developed by Trupti

Vasudev, my co-director, who has embraced the challenges of the changing landscapes of this profession. Presently, Actimedia partners with a global coalition called Travel & Lifestyle Network (TLN), representing them in India, thus forming a large partnership of twenty-four consultancies across forty markets.

We work with lifestyle clients like Fremantle India, Switzerland Tourism, Norwegian Cruise Lines, Blackberrys, DeBeers Forevermark Diamonds and Hyatt Place Aurangabad Airport, among others.

As an organisation, we choose to work with a defined set of clients for whom we do our very best and try to exceed their expectations on all fronts. Our mantra has been: 'Don't run after money, let the money pursue you. You go on doing what you truly love and enjoy!'

Some of the iconic campaigns that we have worked on include: Ariel 'Share the Load' (P&G) for four years, Whisper 'Keep Girls in School', the Kingfisher Swimsuit Calendar for eleven years since its inception, Force India Formula One Team for four years, 'I Need Switzerland' for Switzerland Tourism, Sula Wines, Bira 91 and, most recently, USPA 'Legends Forever Play Together'.

Public Relations in India is Evolving at a Rapid Pace

Corporates still do not utilise their PR firms to their full extent. Most brands consider us partners who get them media visibility and corporate interviews. But we can do so much more than that. Since a large part of the media coverage is paid, lifestyle partnerships are a mix of ads and content through advertorials. The client feels that if they anyway have to pay for coverage, why have a PR firm on board. Of course, these are the problems most consultancies face.

PR firms are not seen for their strategy, positioning and crisis management skills. The perception is that PR companies get only your pictures and story in the newspapers. The value addition of the thought process, the crafting of messages and the inputs on brand equity are overlooked because our profession has historically not put a price on these services. The most common reaction we receive is: if you don't give me your services at a rate I want, I shall move on to another PR firm.

As professionals, we should be engaged to build brand value for the tools deployed, to get that fabulous piece in print or online, or highlight the value that led to an influencer talking about the brand in a light that was derived after much research, data crunching, strategy and careful content creation.

As a collective, the tool-sets of our work life have evolved from landlines to mobiles, faxes to emails, carousel projectors to PowerPoint presentations, hard copies of photographs to digital ones, physical meetings to virtual calls, and now we are seeing the advent of AI in different spaces, starting with content creation.

So while the tools have advanced to better assess our environment and make our jobs easier, the cerebral hard work still remains the same in terms of brand positioning and strategising. It's high time that we receive the right price for these.

24

Radhika Shapoorjee

Founder and CEO, Mediation Mantras

'All relationships can bring love, joy and purpose. Each person contributes and has a role for a truly fulfilling life.'

Transitioning from Advertising and Sales to Public Relations

I was born in Kolkata and had a childhood filled with both love and pain. Till the age of six, I was the first-born adored by everyone from both my parents' families. But my father fell seriously ill and passed away when I was just six years old. He was the most loving, kind, and wonderful person in my life, and losing him at such a tender age was devastating. It was my first experience with grief, though at that age, I couldn't fully comprehend its impact.

My first memories of how grief was handled around me shaped how I responded to difficult situations later in life. In my family, people suppressed their emotions. No one talked about my father, instead pretending that everything was fine. As a child, I could sense the sadness all around me, especially as my young and brave mother coped alone with two very small children. I know now that back then, she simply wanted to get a sense of normalcy in our lives, but to me it felt as though everyone wanted to simply forget the incident and move on.

This early experience taught me my first life lesson, that it doesn't matter what the situation, you must always show up. In fact, after my father's passing, I felt a deep sense of responsibility for my younger brother and my mother, and in a way lost a part of being a child. I naturally gravitated towards helping others, stepping in whenever I sensed trouble, sometimes even if it wasn't my issue to fix. While this instinct to help became a strength, I later learnt the importance of setting boundaries and letting go of unhealthy emotions and being able to say 'no' to people.

My school life was spent at Delhi Public School, RK Puram, where I met my first friends. They became my bedrock of love and friendship. I was also very fortunate to participate in sports, as it helped shape my life. I was a swimmer and runner and played basketball, eventually representing my school at the national level. I met my next group of friends from the basketball community, and they still remain my best friends. Sports taught me teamwork, discipline, resilience and how to handle both victory and defeat. Being a sports captain helped me develop leadership skills early and understand the power of camaraderie and collaboration early in life.

I joined St Stephen's College. College was a joyful phase of my life, filled with friendships. Beneath the fun and freedom, I was driven by a strong desire to become independent and start earning as soon as possible. We had campus placements and I got a job with the Oberoi Hotel in April that year, but the start date got postponed to July. Coincidentally, my childhood friend pointed out a newspaper ad, and I immediately applied for and got a job at UDI Yellow Pages.

My first boss, Arvind Wable, was a remarkable person and a great mentor. He interviewed me, recognised my potential and hired me. Sales felt natural to me, I was hardworking, and the challenges didn't faze me. The heat of summer didn't bother me, as I had played intensive sports in all seasons. I worked harder than anyone else and achieved the highest sales.

This was a defining moment in my life. At a young age of twenty-three, I was put in a leadership position, managing a team of older colleagues. Despite the age difference, I led with confidence, and put my discipline in sports and team camaraderie to work. The institutional team initially worked across large organisations. We then started working closely with advertising agencies, pitching the Yellow Pages concept to them for their clients.

As I did the rounds, I visited Clarion Advertising, where I felt an immediate connection with the world of advertising. Something about the agency felt right, and I knew I wanted to work there even though I didn't have any advertising experience. My persistence to seek an opportunity paid off, and I was offered a job as a senior account executive by Probir Purkayastha, who was heading the agency. Here, I started learning the basics of advertising and working on campaigns around AIDS awareness. It was my introduction to a world I had no prior knowledge of, and I was determined to learn everything I could.

Meanwhile, my mentor, Arvind Wable, had moved to Ulka Advertising (now FCB Ulka) along with the leadership team from UDI Yellow Pages. After six months at Clarion, I reached out to him, expressing my interest in joining Ulka.

He welcomed me into his new team, and I began my journey with Ulka.

My time at Ulka was transformative. From 1992 onwards, I spent nearly nine years immersed in advertising, which was also an incredible time, as India opened up to the world at large. When I joined, the company primarily hired client servicing professionals from the IIMs, so I was surrounded by some of the brightest minds in marketing, including Sanjeev Bhargava, Roy Cherian and Rajeev Shukla, who continue to be dear friends. To keep up and, more importantly, write good briefs, I bought Philip Kotler's marketing textbook, read many issues of the *Harvard Business Review* and taught myself the fundamentals of advertising through self-study.

My first major client was Ravi Kant, the marketing director of LML Vespa (who later went on to join Philips, and then to become the CEO of Tata Motors). Working closely with him for six years on LML Vespa was an invaluable learning experience, as he was referred to as the 'Turnaround Leader'. Advertising taught me the importance of using consumer research to identify problems and solutions that formed the basis of the communication strategy and campaigns. I also learnt the importance of businesses to adapt to a changing external environment. For instance, I witnessed a major shift in the two-wheeler industry when government regulations pushed manufacturers to transition from two-stroke to four-stroke engines. This change destroyed brands like LML, which failed to adapt quickly enough. Watching a once-successful brand collapse taught me how external forces can reshape entire industries.

During my time in advertising, I met my husband Mehernosh Shapoorjee, who was the creative director at Ulka. We worked together for several wonderful years, and then I decided that it was time to explore a different path at work. It was early 2000, I had just had my first child. After a year, with a lot of encouragement from my mother-in-law, I returned to working full time. But I wanted to broaden my horizons beyond advertising. That decision marked the beginning of the next chapter in my career.

I moved to public relations with a clear goal, which was to diversify my professional portfolio by adding PR to my experience in advertising and sales, thereby making myself ready for a corporate role with a client. But that was never to be, as I completely fell in love with the profession over the years. My mentor Arvind proposed that I set up FCB Ulka's PR department in Delhi. I didn't know anything about PR but decided to take the opportunity as a challenge. I started the PR function with one junior associate and collaborated with the direct marketing team. I knew I had to learn fast. To bridge my knowledge gap, I got hold of textbooks on PR and realised that it was quite different from advertising, so I decided to meet with various leaders.

I reached out to heads of consultancies such as IPAN and Genesis, which were the prominent PR firms at that time. I met Prema Sagar at her Genesis PR corporate office in Gurgaon. I explained that I was setting up a PR practice at Ulka and had come to seek advice on the PR domain and the kind of work that they were doing for their clients. She was very generous with her insights. However, I also recognised that the infrastructure and focus of an advertising agency didn't lend itself easily to growing a PR division.

About a week later, Genesis called me back for an interview and offered me a leadership role as a partner associate in the firm. I was delighted, as Prema Sagar trusted my advertising and leadership experience and allocated a talented team of twelve people who were handling nineteen accounts across different sectors. Coming from advertising, where I typically worked on only a few brands at a time, managing so many accounts was a significant but exciting shift.

At Genesis, I was able to apply my knowledge and insights from advertising, which included campaign planning, messaging and even revenue generation strategies with my clients. I was fortunate to spend my initial weeks with the various teams at the New Delhi office to evaluate the scope of work and strategies that governed client work. I realised that campaign planning wasn't common in PR at the time, so I introduced the process to my key clients.

My first client endorsement in PR came from the team at National Geographic Channel. A very special mention to Zubin Gandavia and Dilshad Master, with whom we rolled out the messaging and campaign plan. I'm incredibly grateful to my very talented colleagues including Kanak Pillai, Papri Dev, Deep Ghatak and many more, where we combined our knowledge to create some great campaigns. During this time, I immersed myself in studying PR further and learning from my team and colleagues like Deepshikha Dharmaraj and Sheena Sharma, who were amazing leaders and very generous with their insights. I extensively used the Holmes Report online (now Provoke Media), which had a goldmine of global case studies across industries, to understand the nuances of strategic PR campaigns. It helped me and my team conceptualise many campaigns across clients.

Over the six and a half years at Genesis, I transitioned through various roles, including taking a sabbatical for three years after having my second child, and then I returned as head of strategy and innovation at Genesis Burson-Marsteller. I led the SQI (Service Quality Index) of the top twenty clients, which gave me deep insights on how to deliver service excellence. I put all my combined knowledge of advertising and PR to train the teams across the firm on reputation and brand campaign planning frameworks.

In 2007, I met Colvyn Harris, the CEO of JWT India (now VML India). He inspired me to join IPAN (Indian Public Affairs Network), as vice president and head of new business. Within ten months of joining, he offered me the mandate to head IPAN as president. It was a tough but exciting mandate—I had to find and put in place a new set of leaders across the Delhi, Mumbai and Bangalore offices, as the previous set of leaders had moved on. I went through a process of restructuring the firm by practice and specialisation. We upskilled teams to deliver messaging and campaign plans for clients across the country, which led to winning new businesses and retaining the old clients.

One of the first clients that was retained was Unilever in Mumbai. They were not happy as there had been frequent team changes and wanted to go for a pitch. At IPAN, we had a new and dynamic leader, Vinod Moorthy, who had joined us in the Mumbai office. Together, we negotiated to re-pitch for the eight brands before they called in other consultancies. Ashok Venkatramani, who was leading the personal care brands of Unilever in India, gave us that chance. We identified the most critical areas of concern, restructured the teams and developed unique campaigns to deliver exceptional work for all their eight brands. One standout initiative that we worked on was the 'Lifebuoy Swasthya Chetna Clean City Campaign', aimed at promoting health and hygiene across twenty cities. This campaign was incredibly successful, laying the groundwork for securing and consolidating businesses from Unilever in subsequent years.

This successful retention of a big and important client gave me a sense of confidence to look at shaping an exciting new future for the firm. And then we were faced with the first big corporate crisis and scandal with the fall of Satyam Computers. We had recently signed on the business, and it was seen as a bellwether brand in the IT industry. It was late evening, I was sitting at the Chennai airport and I got a call—there was going to be mayhem the next day, as *The Economic Times* was filing a front-page story about a deal that had gone wrong for Satyam. I can never forget the call that was set up with the entire corporate communication team from across the world the next morning, to discuss the negative headline news, where my question, 'What are the facts around what was reported?' was met with complete silence.

We observed from the sidelines the miraculous reputation recovery of the brand and its acquisition by Tech Mahindra.

It was a lesson on what not to do in a crisis, as it caught us completely off guard. This incident resulted in the setting up of a crisis management practice, which helped us manage many other issues and near-crisis situations very effectively. Personally, it taught me a big lesson to remain calm in a storm. I learnt that truth and transparency are non-negotiable, both in navigating brand challenges and in building long-term trust.

During this trying time, I had connected with Vivian Lines, President APAC at Hill & Knowlton, and he gave me a lot of support and advice during this crisis. It led to a strong association with Hill & Knowlton for a year and then to an integration of IPAN with Hill & Knowlton in 2009. Viv Lines opened the doors of our firm to global clients and best practices and gave us an exposure to the global network across Europe, Asia Pacific, Middle East and the USA. It enhanced the ways of working across geographies and significantly enriched the professional growth of the organisation.

At IPAN Hill+Knowlton Strategies, I was fortunate to lead an amazing team, and together, we created impactful campaigns that left a lasting legacy. I would like to mention one of my most memorable campaigns for Max New York Life (now Axis Max Life Insurance), where the faith and foresight of the leadership team of Gary Bennet, Debasis Sarkar and Abhinav Rahul resulted in building a long-term brand and communication assets. This strategic campaign used a category truth and a consumer insight from the life insurance industry research: 'People only bought life insurance for tax saving measures rather than to protect their family from financial vulnerabilities.' This insight led to the creation of the 'India Protection Quotient' (IPQ), which highlighted the financial vulnerabilities of Indians and educated consumers to address this root cause, thereby promoting the true value of life insurance. It was nominated at the Cannes Festival of PR and advertising and was recognised as a very valuable brand property. It continues as a thought leadership platform even today, over a decade and a half later.

The integration with Hill+Knowlton led to some amazing wins that built a strong reputation for the firm. We won the entire Microsoft mandate for corporate PR, marketing communication and CSR in 2011. This was made possible by the marvellous team including Sara Gourlay, Sudha Sarin, Lavang Khare Richard Price, Neha Bharghav and many more talented teammates who worked for weeks to pitch to the incredible communication leader at Microsoft, Meenu Handa, and her team. This win came after two unsuccessful earlier pitches for the business, and therefore was a very sweet victory.

However, the communication landscape began to evolve rapidly with the rise of social media and its impact on brand reputation. A big wake-up call for us as a team was in 2012, when we lost one of our strongest partnerships—the Unilever account. It became evident that although we excelled in traditional PR, campaign planning and crisis communication, we were struggling to adapt to the rise of social media and its growing significance. We explored collaborations within the WPP system to address this gap, but these efforts were largely unfruitful, as I realised that a digital integration needed to be embedded into the core structure of the consultancy.

I also realised the importance of building a network of people who could be your trusted advisors and help you reflect on the path ahead. I was fortunate to be selected for the Aspen fellowship, which is a global think tank that selects leaders across business, government, NGOs and the legal fraternity and creates a cohort of about twenty leaders. We met every six months for five days, where a very special trust-based bond was built. Being able to get away from the intense cycles of work and home allowed a space where I could self-reflect as well as check in with the lives of the other leaders.

We had discussions around topics that explored our leadership styles, our challenges and how to shape a significant future. It was a journey of how to take your life from success to significance. It had a deep impact on my personal journey, thoughts and actions as I navigated the world of PR. I made new friends who continue to be a part of my life.

By mid-2015, I began to feel a sense of my own leadership inadequacy, as balancing the demands of leading a large consultancy and attempting this transformation proved to be a significant challenge. I was feeling overwhelmed with keeping pace with the changing communications landscape and its impact on clients, my team and the profession. After much introspection, I realised that my time leading a PR consultancy was no longer joyful, and it needed a new leader. I conveyed my decision to step down to the global leadership team and Viv Lines.

My departure was well planned, as I had committed to ensuring a smooth transition, taking a year and a half to identify and onboard my successor, Chetan Mahajan, as the CEO, ably supported by Deepa Jayaraman, who had worked with me over the past ten years. Both were exceptional leaders. I felt a great sense of relief as I bade farewell to an organisation and business that had enriched my life and given me so much, but I knew I wanted something more from the rest of my life.

During this transition, I was very fortunate to connect with the Singapore International Mediation Centre (SIMC), where I met with the leadership team Aloysius Goh and Viswa Sadasivan. They introduced the concept of mediation to me, which was a novel and amicable way to resolve conflicts. This meeting sparked my curiosity and the connection with mediation was instantaneous. They entrusted us with a project to explore the state of mediation in India, including its challenges, opportunities and strategies for implementation.

My husband Mehernosh Shapoorjee, who was now an independent leadership and strategic consultant, joined me on this journey, and together, we collaborated on this project with the H+K team, conducting extensive research and engaging with stakeholders ranging from industry associations to lawyers, general counsels and government representatives. After successfully completing the project with SIMC, my association with IPAN and Hill+Knowlton Strategies came to an official close in late 2017.

This project on mediation led us to a wonderful partnership with SIMC, which recognised our expertise and invited both my husband and me to become India specialist mediators. I have to thank George Lim and Professor Joel Lee for providing comprehensive training for the India cohort of mediators.

And this marked the beginning of a new chapter in my career. I immersed myself in mediation, dedicating nearly two years to rigorous learning. I pursued domestic and international certifications, read over fifty books and developed an India-specific pedagogy that combined communication, psychology and mediation. I had found my true purpose and passion. I had made a full circle from my childhood lessons of suppressed emotions and inability to express to channelling communication as a true force of good in mediation.

In 2019, my husband and I co-founded Mediation Mantras, a venture born out of this journey. It focused on helping individuals and organisations resolve conflicts and build better communication strategies, leveraging the principles of mediation and crisis communication. This transition from PR to mediation was both unexpected and deeply fulfilling. And I viewed it as a gift that has allowed me to explore a completely new realm with huge potential impact to change the adversarial way of win-lose to a win-win collaborative way.

And the most important lesson that I have learnt is that building strong, meaningful relationships is absolutely essential. It's those connections, that support system and the joy you find in those relationships that give you the strength to commit fully to life. Whether it's your partner, your children or your closest friends, every relationship should bring you joy and purpose. When you nurture those bonds, they in turn empower you to chase your goals and dreams wholeheartedly.

A Shift in the PR Business

Over last two decades, those in the PR business have shifted from being mere press relations managers to having a strategic role focused on building and protecting an organisation's reputation at the C-suite level.

I joined the profession in 2001 and observed that PR was driven by media intelligence, press releases, interviews and strong media relations to create a solid news desk for clients. What set PR apart, however, was its ability to anticipate and mitigate bad news. This could range from a misquote, to a negative headline to a continuous cycle of negative breaking news.

The 2008–2009 global financial crisis was a turning point for PR, highlighting the critical role of crisis communication and reputation management. There was a huge trust deficit with big business, as reckless lending led many financial institutions to fail and require government bailout.

In India, the fall of Satyam and its acquisition by Mahindra became a defining lesson for PR and business professionals on crisis recovery and reputation restoration at both organisational and national levels. There have been many a rise and fall of leaders and organisations post this event, but the speed, pace and impact of restoration of reputations is yet to be matched.

In my view, the evolution of the PR business can be summarised as follows:

PR's strategic shift up the value chain: PR consultancies have become essential strategic partners for the C-suite, shaping messaging, conducting media training and ensuring crisis preparedness. Leaders recognise that a CEO's response in the first moments of a crisis can define an organisation's future reputation.

Clients have realised the business impact of long-term investment in reputation management. Most communication leaders have a seat at the table in board rooms, as they bring significant views that influence present and future initiatives of their organisation.

The rise (and fall) of the influencer CEO: Value-based CEOs have built trust and credibility through meaningful communication and humanised their role as leaders. Ratan Tata is the quintessential example of a leader who navigated the trials and tribulations of business and was seen as an impeccable human being. Similarly, CEOs like Anand Mahindra, Kiran Mazumdar-Shaw, Deep Kalra and Deepinder Goyal have gained huge credibility and are looked upon as role models.

However, high-profile downfalls, such as Vijay Mallya and Chanda Kochhar, highlight the risks of overhyped and mismanaged reputation.

Reputation beyond products—Purpose-driven campaigns: Over the years, PR has expanded beyond media relations to build reputation capital through consumer education initiatives, sustainability and CSR. Organisations expanded their corporate communication teams and budgets to build campaigns beyond just their product launches and business performance. They told compelling stories about the larger good and impact on society.

Indian PR consultancies have gained global recognition for their campaigns at Cannes, Spikes Asia and SABRE Awards.

Social media's impact on reputation management: The breakdown of the silos of traditional and social media has transformed reputation management, where a single negative review or complaint can impact a brand as it enters into the news cycle.

PR consultancies now actively monitor brand mentions, manage influencer collaborations, engage directly with consumers and track real-time campaign metrics across platforms like Facebook, Instagram, X and LinkedIn.

However, the need for credibility continues with traditional news, especially the print media, including mainlines, business and the regional media. Interest-based influencers and expert podcasters have become an integral part of the news and media relations cycle too.

Structural changes and integrated services: With PR evolving into a full-service offering, agencies now rival advertising and marketing firms. There has been an ongoing consolidation of PR brands in conglomerates like WPP, Publicis Groupe and at IPG-Omnicom to optimise their teams, services and global reach.

Clients have expanded budgets for specialised services, and consultancies have invested in talent, technology and infrastructure. Today's PR teams include crisis managers, media trainers, campaign strategists, social listeners and regulatory experts.

There has also been an exponential rise in new and different types of clients who need PR. These include NGOs, start-ups and new-age entrepreneurs.

It's also interesting to see that the rise of revenue and profitability of PR consultancies has overtaken that of advertising agencies in the past couple of years, reinforcing its value proposition for clients.

PR has undergone a structural transformation over the last two decades, solidifying its role in building, protecting and even resurrecting reputations. The profession's future is dynamic, with many more transformational shifts on the horizon.

25

Atul Sharma

CEO, Ruder Finn India, and Head, Middle East

'My philosophy is to keep learning, from anyone at any time.'

From a Tiny Village in the Hills to a National Stage

I belong to a tiny village near Theog, a small town roughly 30 kilometres from Shimla, Himachal Pradesh. I grew up around grandparents, cousins, lots of animals and wildlife. My childhood was full of beautiful and spooky memories of the hills, surrounded by pine and cedar trees, gurgling mountain streams and lots of conversations around the fireplace. It did help that I grew up at a time when there weren't any gadgets around. We had a TV in the village and even that refused to work because the terrestrial signals were weak.

During this time, I learnt an important life lesson: When you spend time with people, you listen more, you want to talk to them and you genuinely become interested in people and things around you. I also learnt that if you can think and tell stories, you will go a long way. And if you can learn the language of nature, animals and humans, you can be the ultimate storyteller.

Communications, however, was an odd career choice. Everyone around me wanted to either be an engineer or a doctor. I tried to go down that route as well but, fortunately, things didn't work out that way. I completed my master's degree in business economics from the University of Delhi and pursued a career in economics and research. While it was a fruitful profession, I missed connecting with people like me, and wanted to do something more interesting—where stories could be crafted and told.

It all started with Nikhil Dey, who was speaking at a session on storytelling, at our annual convention of the Department of Business Economics. I loved his speech and stayed in touch with Nikhil. One day when I got bored of my job, I approached him, and he suggested I give PR a try. That changed everything for me.

I started with Clea Public Relations in 2000 as a management trainee, where I was responsible for managing campaigns for Ernst & Young, Barista, Live-In, Crossword, Philips, Emami and Netwala.com. I was a part of the two-member team that worked on the conceptualisation and execution of brand promotions for Live-In, an apparel brand. I then worked with Corporate Voice Weber Shandwick for over two years and successfully created and implemented communications strategies for clients, including Oracle, HCL, UTStarcom, Palm Inc. and Logitech. I planned and managed Oracle's corporate reputation programme exclusively for over a year with pan-India and APAC teams.

My move to Genesis Public Relations in 2004 meant I became a partner associate within two years of joining. My responsibilities included strategic campaign planning, supervising implementation and review, business development, team learning and driving service quality and process orientation. I went on to lead the technology and consumer practice for the northern region. It was a portfolio of over twenty Indian and multinational companies with a thirty-member team. I went on to become the COO there, which is when Ruder Finn tapped me to run their India office.

Several mentors have had a profound impact on my journey. I still learn from every person I meet or work with. My young team members, especially, have taught me how to multitask. So my philosophy is to keep learning—from anyone at any time.

I have worked on great campaigns over the years for multiple brands. Some that stand out are Ola Electric—End ICE Age, Fitbit—Healthy India, and HP—Computer is Personal Again. They have been incredible experiences and I am proud of the results.

The Dramatic Transformation of Public Relations

Over the past two decades, I've had a front-row seat to the dramatic transformation of the PR profession. It's been exciting to see how the practice has evolved from its traditional roots to the dynamic, digital powerhouse it is today. PR has not only adapted to the changing times but has also become a crucial driver of organisational success.

In the early 2000s, PR was primarily about media relations, press releases and managing corporate reputation. The focus was on controlling the narrative through traditional media channels. I remember spending countless hours crafting compelling stories and pitching them to the press, hoping for that elusive media coverage for a client. But with the rise of the internet and social media platforms, everything changed. The power dynamics have shifted as consumers have gained a voice, making it essential for PR professionals to engage in two-way conversations rather than broadcasting messages.

This era also saw the emergence of influencer marketing. Social listening became essential; we had to monitor online conversations and respond promptly to maintain brand messaging. Brands began to leverage the reach and authenticity of influencers to connect with their target audiences in more meaningful ways. And our young leaders have been key in driving these changes. They understand the importance of being transparent, authentic and having a clear purpose in their communication.

Another significant shift has been the integration of technology into PR practices. The advent of data analytics and AI has transformed how we measure the impact of our campaigns and understand audience behaviour. With this, personalisation became centre stage. At my current organisation, we've been at the forefront of this transformation, incorporating AI tools like Microsoft CoPilot to enhance our strategic capabilities. This not only helps us in crafting more personalised and effective campaigns but also predicts trends and ensures we stay ahead of the curve.

The COVID-19 pandemic further accelerated the digital transformation of PR. With in-person events on hold, virtual events, webinars and digital storytelling became essential. By being flexible and innovative in their approach, companies with strong digital strategies managed to keep their brand reputation strong and stay connected with their audiences.

Of late, there has also been a focus on inclusivity and diversity in PR campaigns. Brands realise the need to represent different perspectives and make everyone feel included. This isn't just about meeting expectations but also about creating a sense of belonging and common purpose amongst different stakeholders.

The PR profession has come a long way in the past twenty years. From traditional media relations to digital engagement and AI-driven strategies, the business has transformed significantly.

26

Ashwani Singla

Founding Managing Partner, Astrum

'Building a science-based reputation advisory was always my goal.'

From Hospitality to the World of Reputation Consulting

My journey into public relations began long before I ventured into this field. I grew up in a middle-class family where my father was a public sector employee and my mother a homemaker. My younger brother and I aspired to make an impact beyond the life we had at that time. We wanted to do something that could make a difference. I studied at the Naval Public School in Delhi, where lifelong friendships and a deep sense of discipline and service shaped my character. Like many of my friends, I dreamt of joining the Indian Armed Forces, but life had other plans. My father wanted me to pursue a career in engineering. I was drawn to economics and liberal arts, eventually studying hotel management at the Institute of Hotel Management in Mumbai.

After graduating, I was fortunate to be offered management training programmes at renowned hotel brands such as ITC, Taj and Oberoi. I chose to join ITC along with my best friend Sheila, who eventually also became my life partner. At twenty-seven, I was given the responsibility of leading the front office at ITC Mughal in Agra; I was amongst the youngest department heads in the company at the time. Driven by an innate curiosity to learn and grow in the new liberalised economy, I decided to expand my knowledge and acquire a bachelor's degree in economics, followed by a post-graduate diploma in international business.

Call it serendipity, but a chance encounter with a former ITC colleague who had shifted to PR opened the door to my pivot to this profession. Intrigued by its potential, I joined Mudra PR in Mumbai as a client group manager in the summer of 1995, thus pressing the reset button on my career and acquiring new skills.

In my brief stint at Mudra PR, I started at the bottom and learnt the basics of PR: writing press copy, doing media rounds, distributing news releases, pitching stories and so on. This phase showed me that PR was my true calling. A key career highlight for me was facilitating a mobile-to-mobile call between Analjit Singh, chairman, Maxtouch (now Vi), and Sunil Gavaskar, India's cricketing icon, a first for a private mobile operator in India.

At Mudra, I was presented with an opportunity to be part of the founding team at Clea PR, the PR wing of Clea Advertising, a firm specialising in financial advertising, and the next phase of my most intense learning commenced.

Winning the Coca-Cola Cricket World Cup mandate within the first three months of launching the firm and handling the Miss World 1996 brief for ABCL, managing Michael Jackson's India visit for Wizcraft, stitching together the remit for Arvind Mills and Sanjay Lalbhai's global leadership in Denim to being recognised as one of the top leaders in the profession in just three years was a rollercoaster ride of a lifetime.

The three years at Clea PR were perhaps my most enriching in terms of depth and variety of learning experiences. Working in the trenches with my sleeves rolled up was the perfect immersion in the fast-evolving PR world.

At both Mudra and Clea, I met some amazing clients, colleagues and professionals from across the professional spectrum, and I cherish those friendships.

Joining Genesis PR in early 1998 marked a new and a very different chapter in my career. What looked like a very successful firm from the outside was fraught with some significant challenges. Also, the departure of its two senior partners, my friend, Kevin Sethi, who lost his battle with cancer, and Archana Jain, who went on to establish her own firm, further compounded the existing business hurdles. One of the major issues we encountered was the significant gap between the perception of what we thought we were and what we delivered to our clients.

There were talented professionals who needed a platform to express themselves, finances that had to be straightened, cash that needed to flow instead of being locked in with clients for over six months, operations that urgently had to be streamlined and client campaigns that should have been more result-oriented and strategic. By being the proverbial bulls in a China shop, we implemented critical reforms. To give more focus to setting things straight, I relocated my family from Mumbai to Gurgaon.

Implementing the Balance Score Card (BSC) was a turning point in confronting the reality of our business and taking proactive steps to drive accountability and merit as the basis for our success. Besides the BSC, one of my proudest and most significant investments was developing the Associate Learning Program (ALP), which nurtured young trainees to grow into true-blue professionals and leaders. The efforts paid off, and within six years (1998–2004), we became leaders in the Indian PR space. We helped in establishing PRCAI, with the first director general being sent to the UK to train with the global body; and in 2006, we hosted the ICCO Global Summit in India for the first time.

We planted the sapling of Impact Research and Measurement in 1998, and it went on to become an independent company in 2003.

I transitioned from non-equity partner to a co-promoter and managing director with significant equity in the firm. In 2004, we received a call from Bill Rylance, APAC president of Burson-Marsteller, to explore an affiliation. By 2010, we had successfully concluded the WPP investment for the firm and we became the first independent domestic firm to attract international investment. The next calling of my life was realising my desire for insights-based strategic communications, and I set up PSB (Penn, Schoen & Berland) for WPP as its Asia MD.

Using research to uncover insights into decision-making has been a passion project. I couldn't do this in the early part of my career, perhaps because the idea was ahead of its time. When Mark Penn, then the global CEO of the B-M Group, offered to set up PSB in India and invited me to spearhead it, I saw it as the perfect opportunity to put my passion for research-based consulting to work.

I soon realised that use of research outside its traditional practice in consumer-related work was still at a very nascent stage, and for research to shape public opinion, it needed to be in the C-suite consideration.

During my first year as PSB MD, I met with over a hundred CXOs to advocate the use of research to shape public perception and achieved a mixed bag of success. We did great work for those who believed in it, and the flywheel started to turn.

Over the next five years, we achieved massive successes, in the corporate as well as the political arena. We did work for captains of the industry, and I had the privilege of working with the truly remarkable late Ratan Tata, among other corporate titans. The fact that the firm was profitable from the beginning gave me a lot of satisfaction.

A key highlight was the unique methodology we introduced in the election campaign strategy. Perhaps the most significant was the 2014 general election campaign for the BJP, where we introduced data science-based decision making into its campaign strategy. The success of these campaigns prompted a shift in the corporate world, where businesses that were once reluctant to invest in research started to recognise its value, and I became its zealot advocate.

As PSB went through certain internal challenges, including global leadership changes, I realised it was time for me to launch my own firm. I had initially planned to start Astrum in 2010 but delayed those plans to focus on PSB. The lessons learnt at PSB set the foundation of Astrum, which brought the convergence of the best of research-based consulting and PR to what I call the 'Science of Persuasion'.

In the summer of 2015, I launched Astrum, built on the philosophy of 'the science of persuasion', where strategic communication is rooted in research-driven insights to ethically shape public opinion. At Astrum, our focus is to use insights gleaned from our research to help our clients successfully negotiate the complex landscape of reputation, risk and regulation and stand apart from their nearest competitors.

We are an 'act first, communicate after' consulting firm, the insights we generate inform clients 'what to do' before 'what to say', allowing them the foresight to shape the company's conduct to strengthen its communication. This approach takes me back to where my journey with Harold Burson started when we first met and he said, 'To be seen as good, you must do good.' This profound piece of advice has served as a beacon of clarity in this highly dynamic profession, where building trust, fostering genuine relationships and driving meaningful change have been the cornerstones of my personal and professional growth.

On a personal level, this journey not only shaped my professional identity but also laid the foundation for understanding the broader changes in the field as the convergence of technology and talent drives the new frontiers of innovations and services.

Looking back, I believe my contribution to the profession was not so much about elevating PR as a strategic management tool, or the dedication to structure and systems, but the development of the professionals who have worked with me, have thrived with their own dedication and thanks to the lessons learnt, thus raising the bar of the practice of professional PR in India.

Public Relations Combines Earned, Paid and Owned Media

Over time, I have seen PR begin as a holistic profession, but slowly evolve into an increasingly fragmented business, centred around media endorsements. This shift has led many people to confuse PR with media relations. The advent of the internet and the emergence of digital influencers and content creators as influential voices in the media landscape have further expanded the scope of PR. Today, securing endorsements from these new-age journalists has become an integral part of PR to drive engagement.

While PR has largely been about earning coverage, it has become imperative to expand beyond this definition. The lines between earned, paid and owned media have become fluid, making it necessary to integrate offline and online strategies. Client-owned platforms—such as websites and social media—present valuable opportunities for direct audience communication, while paid collaborations enhance visibility.

In building sustainable reputation, providing authentic and accurate information in an engaging manner continues to hold the key to make informed choices. Interestingly, while the communication media have evolved, from print to TV, radio, podcasts and social media, the essence of PR remains fundamentally the same: building trust-based relationships.

Engaging with younger professionals, I often notice a disconnect between leadership vision and actual practices. Many still prioritise pitching stories, indicating a slow movement towards strategic communication.

To stay relevant, PR must adopt a holistic approach beyond merely earned content, fully leveraging the emerging technologies that allow direct engagement with stakeholders.

A word of caution: while PR has relied on third-party advocacy to build credibility, the new world of direct engagement offers tremendous opportunities but also comes with great responsibility. To stand apart, the currency of the new world will need to be authenticity.

27

Aseem Sood

CEO, Impact Research and Measurement

'My life has been built on connections, compassion and courage.'

The Boy Who Saved His Bus Fare for *Matar Kulcha*

I have been a lifelong resident of Delhi NCR, and my journey has been nothing short of an adventurous cricket match—filled with unexpected bouncers, occasional sixes and a whole lot of partnerships. My story is one of serendipity, determination and, above all, the value of connections.

I was in third grade when life threw my family a googly. My grandfather, a senior official with the railways, passed away. His job had afforded us the luxury of spacious railway accommodations, but after his passing reality hit us hard because we didn't own a home. My father, an engineer at Engineers India Limited, and my mother, a homemaker with a post-graduate degree in political science and proficiency in

Russian, couldn't afford property in Delhi. So, we moved to Faridabad, which back then was practically the Wild West.

Our neighbourhood had only five houses, and it felt like we were marooned on an island. With no siblings, my dog, Sherry, became my best friend. Together, we explored the barren lands and forged friendships with anyone who joined our cricket matches. Whether you bowled like Kapil Dev or fielded like a statue, you were welcome in our games.

Those days taught me the profound value of inclusivity and acceptance. They made me comfortable talking to anyone—be it a CEO or a cab driver—and finding common ground.

Schooling was an adventure of its own. I initially attended Kendriya Vidyalaya at the Air Force Station in Tughlakabad, which meant a daily commute involving two public buses, a long walk and, occasionally, an encounter with monkeys. Those monkeys weren't your average mischief-makers—they were Delhi's original pickpockets. I had to protect my lunchbox and pockets with more vigilance than a banker guarding his vault.

I still remember a kind-hearted conductor who, every Saturday, refused to charge me the 25-paisa fare, saying, '*Tu toh bahut chhota hai* (You're so young).' That money often went into treating myself to *matar kulcha*, my guilty pleasure back then.

By seventh grade, my principal noticed my lonely waits at the bus stop and convinced my father to enrol me in a school closer to home. Transitioning to the English-medium DAV School in Faridabad after years of Hindi education wasn't easy, but my mother's persistence and belief in me made it happen.

After tenth grade, I set my sights on Apeejay School, Faridabad's best institution. I vividly remember visiting the school alone to collect the admission form, only to realise it required my father's signature. My father, stuck in RK Puram, couldn't make it in time, so I did what any resourceful teenager would—I forged his signature. When questioned, I explained the situation and even wrote a declaration that they could cancel my admission if any details were incorrect. Thankfully, they bought my story, and I got in. That bold move was my first lesson in taking initiative and calculated risks.

After school, I had the good fortune of clearing entrance exams for both the College of Business Studies (CBS) and NIT Kurukshetra. While engineering was my family's legacy, I chose CBS to pursue a career in business. CBS was a melting pot of talent and ambition, and it gave me lifelong friendships and even my life partner, Pooja.

My first job was with Perfect Relations, where I worked on PR campaigns. It was here that I noticed a gap—clients often wanted an independent evaluation of PR campaigns, and the idea stuck with me. Fast-forward to my MBA at IMI Delhi, and I turned this idea into a business model. Though venture capitalists weren't convinced at the time, life had other plans. Straight out of campus, I joined the research division of McKinsey & Co., marking my entry into the world of research and analysis. McKinsey is more than just a job—it's an institution and a transformative way of life. Many of the principles and approaches that define my business philosophy today are deeply rooted in the invaluable lessons I learnt during my time there.

In 2004, my senior at Perfect Relations, Bhuvnesh Chawla, introduced me to Prema Sagar and Ashwani Singla, stalwarts who had funded a project called Impact Research. The project wasn't taking off, so I proposed starting afresh while retaining the name. I rebuilt the business from scratch and today, Impact has 152 employees and many clients who have stayed with us since day one.

If there's one thing I've learnt, it's that luck favours those who build relationships. My journey is filled with moments of serendipity—a conductor who showed kindness, a colleague who introduced me to my investors and mentors who believed in me.

Even today, my network is as diverse as my childhood cricket team. Once at the airport, I spent half an hour chatting with an old cricket buddy who was working as a driver for Oberoi Hotels, only to then meet a tech firm CEO from the same flight. Life has a funny way of connecting the dots.

I also owe much of my philosophy to my father, who taught me that 'enough is a decision, not an amount'. This mindset has guided both my personal and professional life, helping me prioritise values over material success.

From a boy saving bus fare for *matar kulcha* to a CEO leading a small but pioneering company, my journey has been extremely rewarding. Along the way, I've learnt to embrace people from all walks of life, take bold risks and, most importantly, stay grounded. The highlight of my career was being elected AMEC (Association for the Measurement and Evaluation of Communication) Chair in 2022, enabling me to serve the organisation at a global level.

Public Relations Has Evolved into a Strategic Management Tool

Public relations has grown far beyond its beginnings from being a simple media-focused role. From primarily managing publicity and sharing information, PR has grown to play a key role in shaping brand reputation, supporting business strategy and handling global challenges. This shows how PR has adapted to changing technology, society and business needs.

From media relations to new services: A decade ago, most PR firms in India earned their revenue by working closely with the media. Today, that has changed. Media relations services now make up only a small part of their income. Instead, PR firms offer a wide range of services like online reputation management, digital campaigns and integrated communication strategies.

Expanding the PR playbook: In the past, PR relied mainly on 'earned' tools, such as getting unpaid media coverage. However, changes in consumer habits, the media landscape and more complex client needs made this approach less effective. Now, PR uses the full PESO model (paid, earned, shared, owned media) to create a bigger impact. This allows us to reach audiences more effectively and achieve stronger results.

PR as a strategic partner: PR is no longer just a support function—it's now a key partner in business decisions. It helps organisations with crisis response, and environmental, social and governance initiatives. PR professionals often work with top executives to predict risks, find opportunities and guide how a company is perceived.

Data-driven PR: Big data and advanced analytics have turned PR into a measurable and precise discipline. PR is no longer about just creating excitement—it's about delivering real business results. News frameworks (like integrated evaluation framework by AMEC) and tools that allow measurement of more meaningful metrics are helping PR professionals show the value of their work better.

This journey shows PR's ability to stay relevant in a fast-changing world. As organisations face new challenges, PR will remain essential in building trust, shaping perceptions and driving success.

28

Rakesh Thukral

CEO, Edelman Asia Pacific

'I have gained invaluable insights into the workings of a large-scale global consultancy while experiencing the evolution of modern communications.'

A Journey of Diverse Experiences

I come from a close-knit family. My late parents, who were born around the time of India's partition, moved to Delhi to build a life together. My father worked tirelessly from an early age to build a business, while my mother had a brief teaching career.

We lived in a joint family for many years. At dinner, we almost always discussed current affairs. These conversations sparked a lasting interest in the world around me. While in my final year of college in Delhi, I had found a job to assist my father. After graduation, I entered the world of communications and PR. Though I regret not having studied further, I compensate by reading extensively.

In 1991, I joined the Indian Public Affairs Network (IPAN), which later became part of Hill+Knowlton Strategies under the WPP Group. It was my first significant role in the communications profession. I immersed myself in media work and client relations, and the business of it all. I learnt on the job and spent fourteen wonderful years at IPAN. I had the privilege of learning from a veteran like Rajiv Desai while working alongside talented colleagues like Meenu Handa.

After IPAN, I co-founded Comma Consulting, where I worked for four years before becoming an independent consultant. During this period, I worked on several projects, including serving as an outreach advisor to the Bureau of Energy Efficiency at the Ministry of Power.

In 2010, I returned to the large consultancy world and joined Edelman to establish their public affairs division. I've held several roles here: COO and then managing director for India and now CEO for the APAC region.

Edelman has been a career-defining experience for me. I have gained invaluable insights into the workings of a large-scale global consultancy while experiencing the evolution of modern communications. I have worked with some of the world's largest companies and contributed to key developments in the corporate world. My career highlights include supporting Indian companies at the Paris COP in 2015, working on the Flipkart–Walmart deal, launching MTV and Channel V in India and partnering with the Tata Group. I value Edelman's culture and its core values. The company continues to shape the future of communications consulting.

My one takeaway from my career is that teamwork is vital in a service business like ours. The goal then is to build a strong team, ensure everyone performs consistently and maintains clarity of thought. Each day also brings opportunities to learn; we just have to be willing.

My journey has been rich with diverse experiences, and I am grateful for having worked with some of the best in this profession. I remain excited about how our business will adapt to the rise of AI and the unprecedented access modern society has to information.

Liberalisation Brought Global PR Practices and Standards

While PR is constantly evolving, its core principles remain the same. PR is about fostering understanding and crafting narratives that promote and protect brands and organisations. These fundamentals haven't changed, only the tools and channels have. India's PR evolution mirrors the country's rise as an economic powerhouse over the past three decades.

Before liberalisation, PR in India focused on media relations, public awareness and government communication. Corporations relied on in-house teams for outreach and publicity. When global corporations and consumerism entered India in the 1990s, modern PR strategies were introduced. They aimed to shape public perception, engage stakeholders and build awareness.

Liberalisation brought global PR practices and standards and raised the bar for the business. The early 2000s tech, financial and retail boom created new clients for PR firms. It also revolutionised PR practices. As Indian IT companies gained fame, they needed global communication strategies. This period also saw the rise of startup culture in India.

India's growing market offers great opportunities. It attracts global communications firms to build a strong presence and share best practices. Many local PR firms have adapted or have partnered with global networks to improve their skills.

The most significant shift has been the integration of digital and social media. PR professionals now navigate social media by managing online reputations and creating content that cuts through the digital noise.

The digital revolution has merged PR, marketing and advertising. Now, PR professionals in India need skills in content marketing, influencer partnerships and SEO—ideas unheard of at the turn of the century. While traditional media is still important, especially in smaller cities, digital platforms and social media influencers are key to engaging diverse audiences. We must adapt our communication strategies to the changing consumption habits of our audience and tailor our content and messages for different platforms and audiences.

As India's economy has grown, so has consumer sophistication. This has increased the focus on corporate social responsibility and purpose-driven communications. PR professionals must now help brands address social issues and show their broader societal value. The core of PR remains unchanged despite new channels and tools. It is to understand audiences, craft authentic messages, drive action, manage reputation and build trust. We achieve this through storytelling and meaningful relationships.

While a lot in this profession has changed, what hasn't—and shouldn't—are curiosity and consistency. They are vital in PR, now more than ever. Curiosity drives professionals to stay ahead of the curve. They want to learn innovative technologies and understand changing consumer behaviours. And consistency builds trust and credibility—essential commodities in the world of PR. The PR profession in India will evolve in the future while carrying forward its timeless core principles.

29

Sarvesh Tiwari

Founder, PR Professionals

'Beyond PR, giving back to society has always been my core value.'

Public Relations Blended with Social Services

I AM HONOURED AND DEEPLY INDEBTED TO GOD FOR choosing Champaran as my birthplace. It's a place that catalysed and changed the destiny of the nation forever as Mahatma Gandhi started his struggle for India's independence from my hometown.

My education till seventh grade took place in a small town called Bettiah. So when I came to Delhi, I witnessed a different world. At the Air Force School, the difference between a small village and the bustling capital city became starkly clear. Everyone spoke English there. I was initially nervous, but on my second day of school, I was invited to speak at the morning assembly. Since I had limited English skills, I spoke in Hindi. While it was unconventional, people did appreciate the confidence I displayed. It left a deep impression on me because I realised the power of standing out and making a mark rather than blending into the crowd.

During my school years, I participated in debates, declamations, quizzes and sports, especially football. I represented the country at the sub-junior level in football tournaments. While my academic performance wasn't stellar, these experiences shaped my leadership and communication skills, laying the foundation of my career.

After TAFS, I attended University of Delhi's Venkateshwara College, where I was actively involved in student politics. My rebellious spirit led me to organise strikes and engage in political activities. I was even offered the Delhi University President ticket by the National Students Union of India, but ultimately, I was drawn towards communication and public service. This interest guided me to Bhartiya Vidya Bhavan, where I pursued a course in mass communication.

I started my career in the media industry, briefly working with a show called *Ankho Dekhi* and Aaj Tak. My long-standing journey in PR began with the Delhi Metro's PR team. I did have an opportunity to join the defence forces, but I chose PR as I am a people's person, and I knew I would thrive in a field that allowed me to interact with and influence others.

In 2011, after my father faced health issues, I resigned from my job with no plans for the future. I spent a month with my parents, which helped me realise that success is not just about professional accomplishments but also about being there for the people who matter. Soon after, I started getting consultancy offers from companies I had worked with, including Rapid Metro and DLF. It was reassuring to know that my work was valued, and I eventually decided to start PR Professionals (PRP) in 2011.

Initially, I worked alone, setting up my office in a small flat in Janakpuri. By 2013, I started hiring, and since then PRP has grown exponentially. At present, we have over 200 employees and more than sixteen offices across the country and abroad. My journey in the profession, interestingly, has been marked by bridging the existing gaps in the PR sector, especially when it comes to media relations. I noticed that while many consultancies were good at presentations, they lacked strong media connections, and I focused on this with great success.

Some of the most remarkable campaigns I've worked on include the Nirbhaya Movement. As the general secretary of the Nirbhaya Jyoti Trust, I played a key role in organising the movement and coining the name 'Nirbhaya', which became a symbol for justice for women in India. We spoke about the critical need for stronger laws and societal change to ensure women's safety and dignity.

Another notable campaign was for the National Hydroelectric Power Corporation's (NHPC) Subansiri hydropower project on the Assam–Arunachal border that had been stalled for years. Despite strong political backing, the project couldn't move forward until NHPC brought me in. We successfully mobilised the community, using local language and dialects, creating self-help groups and engaging the public in a way that rekindled a project people had given up on. This campaign not only saved NHPC ₹3,600 crore annually but also became a case study in crisis management, winning us recognition from *The Economic Times* and several international awards.

One campaign that is closest to my heart is the one where we provided support for the families of martyrs. After the Uri attack in 2016, we adopted the affected families and took on the responsibility of educating their children. This is something we all should strive to do—to honour those who have sacrificed for the nation. It is our national duty to stand by the families of our brave soldiers, and every citizen should feel the responsibility to give back to society in whatever way possible.

Beyond PR, giving back to society has always been my core value. We have also undertaken social initiatives such as organising pilgrimages for senior citizens and building roads and houses for those in need. I have been actively organising events like the Wheelchair IPL through the Para Sports Foundation and the Wheelchair Cricket Association to promote inclusivity. I'm privileged to have the platform to perform these duties.

PR Has Had a Digital Revolution

Over the last two decades, PR has seen a lot of changes. When I started, traditional media like newspapers, radio and TV were the main channels of communication. The focus was on press releases and building relationships with journalists to shape narratives and build reputations.

However, the digital revolution changed everything. Social media platforms gave individuals and organisations direct access to their audiences. This democratisation of communication meant that anyone could share their message, bypassing traditional media gatekeepers. It gave smaller organisations and even individuals a platform to engage with a global audience.

Crisis management has also evolved with time. In today's digital world, crises can erupt and spread within minutes on social media, requiring immediate and strategic responses. PR professionals need to be more agile and proactive in managing reputation and addressing concerns before they escalate.

Another major shift has been the introduction of data analytics. Today, it's not just about storytelling but also about measuring the impact of that story. Tools that track audience engagement, social sentiment and campaign effectiveness have become essential. This data-driven approach has made PR more accountable and has allowed us to refine our strategies on the go.

In essence, PR has moved from being a media-centric profession to a dynamic, digital-first space where direct engagement, data and technology play pivotal roles.

30

Dilip Yadav

Co-founder, First Partners

'Despite my short attention span, I am a perfectionist. I believe in taking on tasks only if they're going to be done exceptionally well.'

From the Shadows of Marketing to the World of Public Relations

I was born and raised in Agra where I completed my schooling at St Peter's College. At home, our family environment was a melting pot of intellectuals. My great-grandfather was a lawyer, famous for being a gold medallist and the first rank holder in law at Agra University, though he was the only student in the faculty at the time! Degrees in those days were signed by the queen of England. My maternal grandfather served as a civil surgeon during the British era. Although I never met either of them, their stories were a key part of my upbringing.

Our household was steeped in literature and intellectual discussion. Dinner table conversations often revolved around history, revolutions and tales of India's independence. My father's elder brother, Rajendra Yadav, a highly celebrated writer in Hindi literature and editor of *Hans*, was one of my childhood heroes.

Growing up, I was surrounded by books—stacks and trunks full of them—which became my treasure trove of knowledge. In those days, without the internet and with school ending early in the afternoon, I spent countless hours reading, developing a deep appreciation for literature, storytelling and understanding the world through the written word.

Later, I pursued my bachelor's degree in statistics from Agra University and a master's degree in business with a specialisation in marketing. I also obtained a master's in statistics from Agra University, where I went for classes in the mornings and worked in the evenings.

My early career, especially my arrival in PR, was a journey of exploration. I was looking for something new, trying to understand where my true interests lay. After completing my MBA, I was hired by an export house in Delhi to handle their marketing. However, the role didn't quite resonate with me. As a rookie, I didn't get much exposure to the buyers or the key business decisions. Most of my work involved coordinating product samples, which I didn't find fulfilling. So, I switched jobs and joined *Amar Ujala*, the second-largest Hindi newspaper in India at the time.

Amar Ujala was rapidly expanding back then, and I had joined a cadre of management trainees they were grooming to manage the newspaper's growth. Expansion for a newspaper in those days meant opening new printing centres across regional markets. This was the way communication started happening via faxes.

For a whole year, I travelled across India, gaining exposure to all aspects of the newspaper business—editorial, distribution and marketing. Regional markets were crucial to our growth and every new edition required its own local team and infrastructure. One of my proudest achievements was introducing a new business model for classified ads, especially for matrimony, job listings and real estate. Classified ads brought instant cash and were a lucrative revenue stream back then. The country was witnessing the telecom boom and PCOs (public call offices) were rapidly mushrooming across cities. These were mom-and-pop outlets, largely underutilised during the day, as callers would queue up during evenings when outstation calling rates dropped. My idea was to appoint these PCOs as classified booking centres. This made access for customers easy, and revenues from classified ads picked up quickly. Our model was adopted nationwide, and PCOs became hotspots for booking ads. It was a significant innovation that stemmed from a simple observation.

However, after some time, I felt the pull towards a different path—the civil services. I left my job and moved from Agra to Delhi to prepare for the Indian Administrative Services exams. I cleared the prelims as well as the University Grants Commission–National Eligibility Test (UGC–NET), which qualified me for a professor's job. However, I was finding it difficult to find accommodation in Delhi, so I applied to the Indian Institute of Mass Communication (IIMC), so I could avail its hostel facilities.

IIMC changed the course of my life. Though I cleared the Mains exam of the civil services too, I wasn't keen on appearing for the interview. That's because I had discovered a new passion—communications. The world of media felt exciting and aligned with my interests, allowing me to connect with stories and information.

By the time I finished my course at IIMC, I had four job offers. One was from the National Informatics Centre for an information officer role, a coveted government position with a starting salary of around ₹14,000–15,000 a month. Another offer came from McCann Erickson for a media planning role, because I had a master's degree in statistics. However, I was interested in client servicing and strategy, instead of crunching numbers. So I passed on that offer.

The third offer was from the corporate communications department of a steel company. But the fourth was the most intriguing—a small, fledgling PR firm called Corporate Voice, which only had four people in its Delhi office. To understand more about the role and the company, I did my research, met several people and learnt that even top advertising experts had little idea about PR. D.K. Bose from JWT, known as the father of media planning, came to my rescure. He told me that PR was a new concept from the West, and he believed it would grow faster than advertising in India. Even though it was the least-paying offer—around ₹5,000 a month—I decided to take the risk, thinking if it didn't work out, I could always move on. I ended up staying at Corporate Voice for twenty years.

This journey mirrored the broader changes happening in India. Liberalisation had taken off, and foreign companies were entering India, largely through joint ventures with Indian companies. Corporate Voice too entered into a joint venture with Weber Shandwick and was renamed Corporate Voice Weber Shandwick. Later, this business transitioned into a fully owned subsidiary of Weber Shandwick.

There was just one computer in the entire office, and everyone would write their press releases by hand before passing them to a typist.

I started as an account executive and left as the managing director of client services of Weber Shandwick India. In an interesting twist, my joining date—13 April 1995—was the same as my last day at the company in 2015. It was a full-circle moment.

At the time of leaving, I wore two hats—I was managing director of client services at Weber Shandwick India, and the founding India managing director of Creation, which is now known as Current Global.

What kept me there for two decades was the variety of work. I have a short attention span and hence thrive on multitasking. I don't function well in linear, regimented environments, which is why I never moved to the corporate side, despite receiving multiple job offers—almost yearly. I discussed several of these opportunities with my bosses, and there were a couple I seriously considered. However, they managed to convince me to stay, largely because I had the freedom to experiment and tackle a wide range of projects.

One guiding principle at Corporate Voice, from CEO Shiv Reddy, resonated deeply with me. He often emphasised that people were more important than clients—because if the right people stayed, we would always find more clients. Clients will always have their own reasons for choosing who they work with, but maintaining a strong team is key. This value system, though conventional, was powerful and kept me rooted in the organisation.

Also, importantly, the diversity of my responsibilities kept things fresh. Since I had been part of the company from its early days, I was entrusted with various mandates. I launched the technology, healthcare, and advocacy practices at Weber Shandwick. Each year brought a new challenge, and I'd build teams from scratch and establish new practices. I was always involved in new initiatives and this constant change meant nothing ever felt repetitive—it was like stepping into a new role with every assignment, and that's what kept me motivated.

Despite my short attention span, I am a perfectionist. I believe in taking on tasks only if they're going to be done exceptionally well. However, perfection can sometimes slow you down, and the desire to ensure your delivery is unmatched comes with a different level of pain. But that's where the fun lies for me.

I hold myself to very high standards, but I have reasonable expectations from my team. I give them a lot of space because people learn best through observation and practice. This freedom works great for self-driven individuals who thrive in that environment. However, for those who need more structure, this space can be difficult to navigate.

My approach to leadership is to maintain high standards for myself and use that as an inspiration for others, encouraging them to think independently and come up with their own ideas. I've seen team members flourish when given the opportunity to dive into new challenges, and I'm always there to support them.

As a leader, I believe in progress—the way it applies to all groups, whether businesses or families. A progressive family is one where the next generation is smarter, more successful and earns more than the previous one. If that progress doesn't happen, the family, much like a business, starts to decay. That's why I tell everyone who works with me that their goal should be to surpass the older generation, to be smarter and more capable.

One essential leadership trait, which is unfortunately not as common, is clarity. Many times, I find that people, both at the consultancy and on the client side, don't have a clear idea of what they want. Without clarity, you can't lead effectively—just like a general who doesn't know where to send the troops. Clear direction is critical to ensure that your team can deliver what's expected.

I have been a part of some interesting campaigns. In 1996, McDonald's opened its first outlet in India at Vasant Vihar in Delhi, and I was part of the PR team managing the launch. My role was to stand outside the restaurant and act as a media gatekeeper—controlling which media entered, who was photographing and who was lingering. The environment was highly sensitive at that time because of the opposition multinationals entering the Indian food space were facing.

Before McDonald's, KFC had already faced resistance, with its Bangalore outlet being vandalised. Naturally, McDonald's was apprehensive too. For about a year leading up to the launch, only a few people, including myself, were privy to the intricate details of the preparations. When the day finally came, we succeeded in delivering a peaceful, incident-free opening, with extensive national and international media coverage.

In one instance, we faced opposition in Vile Parle, Mumbai, where a Hindu religious group objected to the restaurant opening near their temple. For weeks, the restaurant sat ready but unopened due to the community's resistance. There was a breakdown in communication between McDonald's and the religious group. I was tasked with uncovering the root of the issue. To do so, I disguised myself in traditional attire and infiltrated their meeting at the temple to understand their concerns.

What I learnt was fascinating—what troubled the community was that the vegetarian and non-vegetarian burgers looked identical. They feared their children might accidentally consume meat, which could lead them to develop a taste for it and abandon vegetarianism. This key insight shaped our strategy. Instead of escalating the situation or seeking police intervention, we focused on educating the community.

We created highly detailed infographics and handouts that illustrated the differences between the vegetarian and non-vegetarian sections of McDonald's. The leaflet explained everything—from the different wrappers and apron colours worn by the staff, to how vegetarian and non-vegetarian burgers were stored separately. It even detailed that vegetarian burgers were placed on the top tray, with the non-vegetarian ones below. This approach became a case study in stakeholder communication. It wasn't about fighting the opposition but understanding their concerns and addressing them directly.

Often, consumers can't articulate what they want. You need to dig deeper by engaging with them in more relaxed settings. Most of my valuable insights, and resultant strategies, on important assignments have come from grassroots-level conversations.

New Holland Tractors was a client that was facing a sales challenge. They were producing large, powerful tractors that no one was buying—essentially the equivalent of launching a luxury car in a market where most people only buy small, practical vehicles. Customers couldn't see the value or benefit of purchasing such large, expensive equipment.

The marketing team approached us, saying, 'We need a deep understanding of what's happening here.' I suggested that the only way to truly grasp the issue was to talk directly to customers. Advertising in newspapers about the tractor's superior engineering wasn't going to cut it. So, I decided to go on a field trip to Punjab.

I hired a car and, with no one from the team keen to join me, only managed to get my secretary, who later became a successful marketer and businessman, to come along. We spent a week talking to farmers in the agricultural heartland. The insights we gathered were eye-opening.

We discovered that these large tractors wouldn't be bought for utility—they would be purchased to make a statement. Farmers who bought them were gifting the tractors during wedding ceremonies as a symbol of status, rather than for fieldwork. So, we shifted the entire communication strategy. We began focusing on the marriage season, profiling gifting stories of tractors during weddings. The strategy was highly localised, with regional coverage that highlighted these extravagant tractor gifts, complete with garlands, fanfare and celebrations. And with that, the message was clear: a New Holland tractor wasn't just a machine; it was a symbol of pride and status. The moment we tapped into this cultural nuance, sales began to soar.

This is what I consider real PR—discovering the key insight that drives behaviour and shaping the communication to deliver impact. These examples are a testament to how understanding your audience at a granular level can completely transform a campaign. Although the media mix and the technology environment has changed over years, these customer insight principles still hold true.

Public Relations in the Information Economy

Over the past two decades, PR has evolved from a supporting act in marketing to a central pillar in strategic communication.

As the world shifted from an industrial economy to an information economy, PR adapted, shedding its old reputation of managing press releases and publicity stunts to becoming the guardian of brand narratives and corporate reputations.

Twenty years ago, PR was often subsumed under marketing, with chief marketing officers as its primary clients. Today, PR is managed by chief communication officers, reflecting its distinct and elevated role. PR is no longer about merely amplifying marketing campaigns. Instead, it's about shaping the voice of an organisation across internal and external channels, managing crises and aligning brand values with the evolving social landscape.

This shift stems from a deeper understanding: PR is not just about what a brand sells—it's about what a brand stands for. Companies today are judged by their values, social impact and environmental consciousness. PR professionals curate these stories, ensuring they resonate with modern audiences who demand authenticity and accountability.

Traditional media outlets, once the gatekeepers of public discourse, have been overtaken by the rise of the creator economy. PR is no longer confined to securing a headline in a major publication. Today's equity is also being driven by individual creators, bloggers and influencers who command loyal, niche audiences.

This shift has fundamentally changed how PR operates. Micro-influencers and independent creators are now integral to campaigns, offering brands a direct line to engaged communities.

Digitisation has been the most disruptive force in PR. Initially dominated by advertising and marketing, the digital sphere is now a battleground for PR as well. Online reputations are fragile, and the speed of digital information means crises can escalate in minutes. PR professionals have had to pivot, mastering digital tools like social media management, online crisis response and SEO.

Real-time engagement is now a core PR function. The days of relying solely on earned media are over. Social listening tools and analytics allow PR teams to monitor brand sentiment and respond immediately to online conversations, reshaping strategies on the fly. In many ways, digital PR has become the modern frontline of communication, ensuring that a brand's voice is consistent across all digital touchpoints.

Perhaps the most profound evolution in PR is in its messaging. In the early 2000s, PR was often about promoting business metrics—profits, market share, product launches. But today's audiences are more sophisticated and value-driven.

Today's PR professionals craft narratives that highlight social impact, sustainability, diversity and purpose. Economic growth is no longer the sole narrative. Brands must demonstrate their contributions to society, whether through environmental initiatives or social justice efforts.

PR's transformation over the past two decades reflects broader economic and technological shifts. From its emergence as an independent function to its embrace of the creator economy and digital platforms, PR has become an indispensable force in shaping how organisations are perceived in a hyper-connected world. More than ever, PR strategies have to focus on creating influence, building trust and ensuring relevance in a rapidly changing landscape more than ever before.

ACKNOWLEDGEMENTS

WE HAVE THANKED OUR FAMILIES AND COLLEAGUES IN the first book, Spark. We remain grateful to them always.

A word of appreciation to Westland for believing in the concept of this book and helping us bring it to life. Their support was instrumental in curating this magnum opus of thirty chapters, each unique, each told from the heart. Thanks to boss lady Karthika, editor Aurodeep, marketing honcho Amrita and cover designer Saurabh.

As we did with the first book, we are 'giving back' to the profession and the community. We had created Sparkle Gift Cards in 2023 under a Section 8 company. We have decided that most of the proceeds from this book will go towards supporting the administrative expenses on the company that manages Sparkle Gift Cards. We hope you make sparklegiftcards.com a way of life and support valuable causes in the process.

We will also share our signing bonus as a scholarship with two deserving students of public relations later this year, in memory of our respective fathers who watch over us, the late Anil Salian and the late Sukhdeep Prabhu.